WHERE TWO ARE GATHERED

STORIES OF 12 SMALL CHRISTIAN COMMUNITIES

WHERE TWO ARE GATHERED
STORIES OF 12 SMALL CHRISTIAN COMMUNITIES

Margaret O'Connell Bisgrove

Saint Mary's Press
Christian Brothers Publications
Winona, Minnesota

For my parents,
Clara and Francis O'Connell

Genuine recycled paper with 10% post-consumer waste.
Printed with soy-based ink.

The publishing team included Carl Koch, development editor; Laurie A.
Berg, copy editor; Alan S. Hanson, production editor and typesetter;
Maurine R. Twait, art director; Kent Linder, cover designer; Vicki Shuck,
cover illustrator; pre-press, printing, and binding by the graphics division
of Saint Mary's Press.

The acknowledgments continue on page 158.

Printed in the United States of America

Printing: 9 8 7 6 5 4 3 2 1

Year: 2005 04 03 02 01 00 99 98 97

ISBN 0-88489-499-1

CONTENTS

Preface   7

Introduction   9

Part A   19

The Power of Invitation   21
Small Faith Community 15, Edmond, Oklahoma

Moving from Group to Community   32
The Small Group of Large Faith, Edmond, Oklahoma

Graceful Facilitation   41
The Thursday Morning Group, Orange Park, Florida

Neighborly Love, Family Style   52
Saint Martin DePorres Small Christian Communities,
New Haven, Connecticut

Rites of Passage   61
The Faith Family Small Church Community,
Denver, Colorado

Contemplatives in Action   72
The Mission Group, Dayton, Ohio

Christian Formation   85
SSFRE, Second Sunday Family Religious Education,
Eldersburg, Maryland

Sharing Life and Saying Good-Bye   97
The Emmanuel Community, Sykesville, Maryland

Part B *111*

Church in the Twenty-First Century? *113*
  Communitas, Washington, D.C.

From Rage to Reverence *122*
  The Community of Jesus Our Brother,
  San Jose, California

Back to the Future *132*
  House Church, New Orleans, Louisiana

Mission Possible *141*
  SCCs: Lodi and Acampo, California,
  and Chihuahua, Mexico

Epilogue *151*

Select Bibliography *153*

PREFACE

My gratitude goes to several people who have encouraged me to write about Small Christian Communities over the years. Gloria Thomas, PhD, was director of religious education in my New Jersey parish; at the time, she suggested I write a book. I could not for the life of me see why. Years later Msgr. Tom Caroluzza and I were in a quick-moving line at the University of Notre Dame. Having read a series of articles I had written for my column in *Today's Parish* magazine, he said over his shoulder as we went our separate ways, "I'm telling you to write more." I just kept moving. A couple of years passed until I was in Rochester, New York, giving a keynote address and workshop. At the end of the day, as I headed to my car in the parking lot, a young girl came running up to me and asked me for the titles of the books I had written. I said I hadn't written any. She said, "You should." I asked, "Why?" She replied, "Because it could help someone."

That convinced me. But I still didn't act on it. Maybe it wasn't the right time. I hope this time is the right time in the eyes of both those who have invited and encouraged me and those who might benefit from the wisdom shared by the communities. Many thanks to Barb Darling for her faith in me, and to my editor, Carl Koch, for the opportunity and his continued belief, encouragement, humor, and skill in making real what looks like possibility.

My deepest gratitude goes especially to the Small Christian Communities who took the time and risk to share their stories. They are people of faith, filled with hopeful expectation and a desire to serve other communities by sharing their birthing processes. They did so generously, openly, and honestly, without trying to lacquer their sharing table with layers of polish. The grain of their stories milled is real in our time and grist for the future. I am extremely humbled by their faith, hope, and courage. They remind me that we share sacred ground as church.

Readers will note that I use only first names in most of the stories. This was done for simplicity and readability. I thank members of the communities for allowing me to do this. One community, the Faith Family, asked me to change their names for reasons of confidentiality. I have done so with gratitude. In the few instances in which I have used full names, this was done for clarity.

A special thanks to Msgr. Jack McDermott, who taught me how to facilitate a core team for Small Christian Community formation and helped me to understand that each person's story is part of the larger Jesus Story. My heartfelt thanks extend especially to Patrick Curry, Susi Mosling, Kathy Reiss, and Ann Louise Devine for reading drafts and giving valuable feedback, and to our friends and companions on the journey in Small Christian Community: Joan and Ed McCarthy, Carole Curry, Bob and Bobbie McGrail, JoAnn and Frank Leanza, and Mike Grottola.

Lasting thanks goes to my family, Megan, Christy, and Dan, and my extended larger family for their patience and prayers, pride and hope. Without them I would be a very different story. And surely a much less joyful one.

INTRODUCTION

> [Forty] percent of Americans belong to a small group. . . .
> They're turning to each other for meaning and looking both
> horizontally—toward one another—and vertically—toward
> God—to find understanding in regard to our existence.
>
> (1993 Gallup survey, as reported in *America,*
> 26 October 1996, p. 20)

One estimate claims that four million U.S. Catholics belong to a
small group. Others say that four million is a conservative figure.
We only have to look around to discover that U.S. Catholics in increasing numbers are forming small communities of faith.

Communities are gathering for a variety of reasons too com-
plex to be stated easily. Whatever the reasons, they are forming
and becoming a dynamic presence in the church.

This book profiles twelve Small Christian Communities in an
attempt to understand why they gather, what holds them together,
how they face challenges and discern their purpose, and what
they offer one another, the church, and society.

Rather than attempting an analysis, each profile is drawn
from the stories of community members. These stories form the
larger story of the community. Once each profile was written, it
was sent back to the community for comment and revision. Every
community's story is part of the larger story being written today
by hundreds of Small Christian Communities renewing the universal community of faith, the People of God.

Every story is an invitation to grace. The invitation to share
story often comes by a quick comment like, "We meet on Monday
nights. Come. We'd love to see you!" The people who show up
for Small Christian Community gatherings bring wounds, confusion, or loneliness wrapped in shreds of hope. They come with

joy, insight, and friendship, shrouded perhaps in anger. When the group gathers, the very act of listening and sharing echoes Christ's message in John 15:12: "'Love one another as I have loved you.'" And that is the basis for these stories.

Where people are gathered and centered in Christ, we hear little or big stories of love. If you do nothing else while reading these stories of Small Church Communities, ponder how most of them tell of Christian love. You may be changed, as I have been, by attending to the stories.

TELLING IT LIKE IT IS

I have tried to relate each community's story as it is. In starting the journey, I selected Small Church Communities at random, not because they are perfect but because they have been maturing for a while—from between two and thirty years. I also selected them because someone in their area noticed them. The profiles are not meant to be inclusive of the best Small Church Communities in the country. The community members are imperfect people belonging to an imperfect church in an imperfect world.

These profiles are a simple way for Small Church Communities to get to know a wider range of other communities. It is an opportunity to learn from their experience and perhaps to try something that has worked in Ohio or Oklahoma, California or Louisiana. This is a grassroots book. I began by listening to the experiences of the communities. I had no idea what I would hear. Each community has its own unique history of struggles and triumphs, its own identity and way of being church.

I have been involved with small groups and Small Christian Communities in every aspect of their formation and life together since the 1970s, whether in my local parish, regionally, nationally, or with international Small Christian Community friends. During all those years, the environment that has most influenced me for the better is my own Small Christian Community. My involvement in leadership development and training has been a small offering back to the Holy Spirit, with thanks for all the people with whom I have shared a brief path long enough for their hope, challenges, and wisdom to change me.

I hoped that my experience might be an asset to this process, not a drawback to listening with integrity. I decided to offer the project to the Holy Spirit, but with more than a little doubt attached. I wondered if I would mentally find myself slotting people and communities into categories as I listened. What saved me from my self-made worries was the memory over and over again that it is the people, always the people, acting through the Spirit, with the Spirit, and in the Spirit, who are the personal and community love story. All these people are stories of praise and honor given back to God.

BEAUTIFUL AMATEURS

This book is about amateurs. We may often think of "amateur" in a pejorative way. But in this case, it is the highest compliment I can give. Parker J. Palmer, in *The Promise of Paradox,* states:

> A community consists not of specialized professionals but of generalized amateurs. It is worth recalling the root meaning of that word "amateur"—it means "lover" or "to love." Love is finally the source of all abundance in life, and it is only when love flows from us that the abundance becomes clear. The key to curing is caring, and it seems more and more obvious that the diseases of our time will be cured not by mere professionals who keep their services scarce, but by an abundance of amateurs who care. (P. 108)

All the people involved in these stories of Small Christian Communities are wonderful amateurs in imitation of the house churches of the first centuries after Christ's death. At that time the institutional church had not formed. All these communities had was the memory of the Living Word of God: Jesus. The early Christian communities gathered to remember who Jesus was and what he did. He was the model for the Christian way to love and act.

For centuries we have continued the rememberings. In accord with Vatican Council II, we began to initiate processes of reflective sharing through connecting faith and life. The growing emphasis and encouragement was for the People of God to take personal initiative in becoming mature adult Catholics, able to discern matters of conscience from an informed knowledge and from hearts filled with right motives. The People of God are ordinary people who, through the process of gathering and reflecting, summon up courage and hope that lead to believing more deeply in ourselves and the possibility of God's Reign.

All the people in the communities profiled here are beautiful amateurs-as-lovers. I want to honor their story and the Christ in their midst in an effort to serve a larger, common good. While each story is unique, sometimes I would come away from listening to their audiotape, watching their video, visiting with them in person or by phone, and wonder: What's the story? What I already knew but have realized once again is that every community history is actually quite different. There isn't just one story with a headline and an angle. Each person is a gospel in our time.

By just being with the people and their stories, I marvel at the invitations, hospitality, problem solving, or action for justice and peace I encountered. Sometimes the community doors are closed temporarily, but most often they stand open to foster love passing beyond them to a larger world.

NEVER A STATIC STORY

One of the key reasons people seek out small community is because they feel anonymous in the large church. And one reason small community works in the long run is that the participants realize they could not gather and reflect in the same way at the large parish Mass.

We learn from listening to people's experiences. These stories reflect the joy, pain, and questions of real lives. After all, we usually live life as we stumble through it, and understand it on looking back. In the place where we hear one another's evolving stories, sudden insight often happens. Remarkably, in the telling of story, we finally understand what a moment ten or twenty years ago really meant. And that is revelation.

A story is never static. The details might be repeated, but the meaning changes as we change. In the telling of our stories, we learn what makes us similar, connected, and beyond the desolation of separateness from one another. Stories told in Small Church Communities are the romance language of our time. It is a very old language, but through it we can once again fall in love with life, with Jesus, and with hope in his promises. It is a Trinitarian process. We are not meant to exist alone and unconnected. Neither was Jesus.

The stories of small communities sound like what we hear at a family reunion. As one person retells a story, other family members might look at one another and wonder if they are in the same family because the story varies from their version. Stories are a mixture of fact and meaning. The stories are told with good intentions, are equally true and genuinely sincere. They are based on the family member's experience of the event, not just the facts. Story changes everybody, and everybody changes the story.

Storytelling does create a privileged common ground, a sacrament of presence. In the listening moment, we are host, just as surely as Jesus is in the moment of extending his presence. He promises, "'Where two or three are gathered in my name, I am there among them'" (Matthew 18:20). Reflective sharing and remembering connects us to the Jesus Story, and transforms us. We see and hear differently. We understand differently. With time, we act differently.

THE SPIRIT IS HARDY

Conflicts will be part of any story, and these communities are no exception. Each of the communities in this book has experienced pain, a given ingredient that comes with life as a person and as a community. Yet the communities also provide the opportunity for healing and growth. In these stories you will meet people who experienced criticism, rejection, problems, unsuspected strength, newfound faith, rekindled hope, love, loss, beginnings, courage, loneliness, and the end of loneliness.

While listening to these stories, I realized again that the human spirit is anything but fragile. The human body or the Body of Christ survives by balancing and rebalancing. And God does not wait to bless us until we have our act together. God knows we need help to change and grow at all the corners we turn or brick walls we run into.

Some of the communities have experienced a dark side of the church, of themselves, or of pastoral ministers. For most of the communities, this darkness was not an ending but a beginning, a Genesis moment. I remember a story that Loren Eiseley told about a man in Costabel who walked on the shore between the dark night and the morning light. As the man walked along, he bent down and picked up every starfish washed ashore that he could find. He threw each back into the nourishing sea, saving it from the hands of townspeople who would sell the starfish to tourists. Eiseley named the man the Star Thrower. When asked why he wasted his time doing this when so many starfish still died, he replied that returning another starfish into the sea may not make much difference to a lot of people, but it makes a lot of difference to the starfish.

One person makes a difference by choosing life-giving action, even if the action is one of simple mercy. Indeed, the characteristic I most notice in Small Church Community people is humility. They are out there at dawn, just doing what God's mercy calls for, and often no one but Jesus notices.

Also, people in small communities usually show a willingness to be open and tolerant of uncertainty. Rabbi Harold Kushner, referring to his belief that you do not have to be perfect to be loved, says that married love is not about romance but forgiveness. Mature love sees the faults and is capable of loving flawed people. The Small Christian Communities in these stories see the faults but still embrace the church—though not at the expense of their God-given call to personal conscience.

I thank these People of God for their courage and desire to share their stories to help other communities. The Catholic church is a rich tapestry of wisdom, service, pain, and dysfunction. The early Christian communities struggled just as these contemporary communities do. When communities are seen through the lens of history, we see transformation in crisis and transcendence through holy lives. The experiences shared by these Small Church Communities are such epiphanies. My hope is that you will glimpse the Holy Spirit at work in these stories and in your personal and small community epiphanies.

How to Use This Book

I hope that you will use this book as a resource both to affirm the community you are already building and as a challenge to consider new ways of being and creating community. Each chapter models a small-community style of meeting based on faith sharing.

The term used for Small Christian Communities varies depending on the region of the world in which it is being used. Most of the communities profiled in this book prefer one of three terms: *Small Faith Community (SFC)* is used interchangeably with *Small Christian Community (SCC)* and *Small Church Community (SCC)*. Each term implies that the people meeting together regularly have gone beyond the initial stages of gathering as a small group to a more mature stage of being church in microcosm as Small Church Communities.

Some communities are parish based and some are not. Both are included in these profiles. Small Christian Communities in most of the stories are composed of eight or more people who gather weekly, bimonthly, or monthly in the style of the early church. The SCC is the church in microcosm.

An SCC grounds itself in the practice of four essential elements of church lived by our ancestors. In *Dangerous Memories,* Bernard Lee, SM, and Michael Cowan show how the early Christians gathered in house churches and practiced these essential elements: prayer and ritual—*leitourgia;* community—*koinonia;* Gospel—*kerygma;* and service—*diakonia*. Christian leaders received their formation in the house churches, and the earliest Christian theology came directly from reflection on the Christian life experience of the community. They had the word of God, one another, and the events of daily life from which to draw strength and discern direction. Each of the communities profiled incorporates these essentials rather differently. Each story invites you to reflect on their practice and your practice of prayer and ritual, Gospel, community, and service.

You might want to scripturally revisit the church of the first centuries, alone or with your community. Some references to the early house churches include the home of Stephanas of Corinth (1 Corinthians 1:16; 16:15–17), Phoebe's house in Cenchreae (Romans 16:1–2), the community gathered with Priscilla and Aquila in house churches in Corinth, Ephesus, and Rome (Acts, chapters 18 and 19; 1 Corinthians 16:19; Romans 16:3; and 2 Timothy 4:19). Keep these early communities in mind as you reflect on the stories here.

Another helpful guide to use in reflecting on these stories and on the story of your community is the statement from the U.S. Bishops' Committee on Hispanic Affairs, *Communion and Mission*. Although it is a guide for bishops and pastoral leaders on Small Church Communities, every community can easily use it. The questions are excellent as both a guide and an evaluation tool for use as the community develops and grows.

For ease of use, each chapter of this book is formatted to include prayer, Good News both from the Scriptures and from a community story, and questions for reflection and community sharing. Generally, I recommend that the questions be reflected upon first by groups of three. Then the small groups can join with the whole community for further faith sharing. Please encourage all community members to raise their own questions about the stories, too.

Facilitators, core teams, and parish staffs can easily adapt a chapter into a workshop setting for educational purposes in a faith-sharing style. Rather than try to finish a story and reflection at one meeting, it may help to spread the reflection time over the length of two or more gatherings. Your community deserves ample time to break apart the words on the page and connect them to faith and daily life.

Adapt the book to your situation. The stories and reflection questions are only starting points for faith sharing. If you do not find the questions in the book pertinent, these two questions would do nicely: The essential formation question is, "What is the Spirit calling me to see and understand in this story?" The essential community question is, "What is the Spirit calling us to do?" Concentrate on faith sharing that connects and weaves together faith and life. Solely intellectual debate can too easily bypass personal reflection. Faith sharing is an opportunity for dialog and prayerful insight.

LET US BEGIN

Clarissa Pinkola Estés in *The Gift of Story* remarks:

> In our present time, there is a goodness to, and a necessity for, rugged independence among individuals. But this is often best served and supported in good measure by deliberate interdependence with a community of other souls. Some say that community is based on blood ties, sometimes dictated by choice, sometimes by necessity. And while this is quite true, the immeasurably stronger gravitational field that holds a group together is their stories . . . the common and simple ones they share with one another.
>
> Though these may revolve around crises tamed, tragedy averted, death be not denied, help arriving at the last moment, foolish undertakings, hilarity unbounded and so on—the tales people tell one another weave a strong fabric that can warm the coldest emotional or spiritual nights. So the stories that rise up out of the group become, over time, both extremely personal and quite eternal, for they take on a life of their own when told over and over again.
>
> Whether you are an old family, a new family or a family in the making, whether you be lover or friend, it is the experiences you share with others and the stories that you tell about those experiences afterward, and the tales you bring from the past and future that create the ultimate bond.
>
> There is no right or wrong way to tell a story. Perhaps you will forget the beginning, or the middle or the end. But a little piece of sunrise through a small window can lift the heart regardless. So cajole the old grumpy ones to tell their best memories. Ask the little ones their happiest moments. Ask the teenagers the scariest times of their lives. Give the old ones the floor. Go all around the circle, and coax out the introverts. Ask each person. You will see. Everyone will be warmed, sustained by the circle of stories you create together.
>
> Though none of us will live forever, the stories can. As long as one soul remains who can tell the story, and that by the recounting of the tale, the greater forces of love, mercy,

generosity and strength are continuously called into being in the world, I promise you . . . it will be enough. (Pp. 28–30)

And so, let us begin.

PART A

The first eight communities profiled are all *parish-based communities*. In general, this means that they are connected to a parish that may be organized as a community of small communities.

Often the parish will have a *core team* to guide the communities' relationship to the larger parish. Members of the core team are usually selected in one of two ways: one, by the pastor, staff person, or coordinator of Small Christian Communities; or two, by being elected or chosen by her or his community.

In a number of the communities profiled in Part A, the core team member will also be the designated *facilitator* or *pastoral facilitator* of the community. The facilitator's role varies, but, in essence, this person serves as the link between the parish and the SCC that is part of the parish. Within the small community, the facilitator may encourage faith sharing, invite the members to share their gifts and skills for the good of the community, and affirm and challenge the community during stages of growth and development. Some of the facilitator's most important tasks include being a person of prayer and hospitality, being a good listener, and offering Christian kindness.

As these stories make clear, just because communities are parish based does not mean that they are carbon copies. Each community has its own character and charism, tensions and virtues.

THE POWER OF INVITATION

Small Faith Community 15
Edmond, Oklahoma

Gracious God, we thank you for the many ways you have called us by name. Help us to bear your name and message honorably, without arrogance, puffed-up pride, or misguided authority. Help us to be Christ for others. Whether we bear good news or messages hard to speak and harder to hear, we ask your guidance at all times, and we praise your name forever.

GOOD NEWS FROM JEREMIAH 1:4–10

Now the word of the LORD came to me saying,
> "Before I formed you in the womb I knew you,
> and before you were born I consecrated you;
> I appointed you a prophet to the nations."

Then I said, "Ah, Lord GOD! Truly I do not know how to speak, for I am only a boy." But the LORD said to me,
> "Do not say, 'I am only a boy';
> for you shall go to all to whom I send you,
> and you shall speak whatever I command you,
> Do not be afraid of them,
> for I am with you to deliver you,
>> says the LORD."

Then the LORD put out his hand and touched my mouth; and the LORD said to me,
> "Now I have put my words in your mouth.
> See, today I appoint you over nations and over
>> kingdoms,
> to pluck up and to pull down,
> to destroy and to overthrow,
> to build and to plant."

THE STORY OF SMALL FAITH COMMUNITY 15

Carol, born and raised in Oklahoma, remembers when nearby Oklahoma City was a small community. "There weren't too many Catholics. We went to Catholic school and that was the nucleus of our social life. It used to be a quiet little town nestled in a territory that became a state in 1907 by means of a land run. 'Oklahoma' means Land of the Red Man. Today, Native Americans living in about sixty-three tribes, are still central to Oklahoma's history. They are quiet, good people who have great care for the environment and Mother Earth. The dirt is red here, and, like it or not, tornadoes come right alongside oil, wind, and rose rock. And if you don't like the weather, stick around. It'll change in five minutes.

"Now, Oklahoma City is big," continued Carol. "When we had the horrible bombing in 1995, it brought back to me the old feeling of what the city used to be like. It was a community that pulled together and helped one another. Oklahomans are really wonderful people, and it's a great place to live!"

"Y'all come!" is an everyday phrase here. SFC 15 belongs to a parish where "Y'all come!" is real. One-third of the parish moves approximately every two years. Edmond, Oklahoma is a city where many upper-level managers live. Boards of organizations always have seats open because people come and go so much. Even so, Saint John's parish opened a Catholic grade school recently, rather than closing one. The parish is welcoming and hospitable. Saint John's has around forty Small Faith Communities, with some communities always in transition.

The rate of job transfers of parishioners is slowing, but Small Faith Community 15 has shaped a pattern for life together that allows for the shifts in membership. When the parish began establishing the small communities, initially they just gave each one a number. SFC 15 decided just to keep the number for their name. They knew who they were and did not feel the need for a special name. The community is now twelve years old. Ages in the group range from three to sixty-four years. The membership has varied in number over the years from ten to twenty-four.

Inviting and Belonging

Given the flux among parishioners, and yet the desire to be hospitable and inviting, questions of welcoming new members always seem to be an issue in the parish's communities. The dilemma is no different for SFC 15. "Some groups don't reach out to newcomers because they like the comfort of being together," said Carol. New members mean that a group has to stop, retell its story, and bring the new people up to speed about the community and all the members. New members also change the dynamics because they bring new gifts, new perspectives, and new foibles. SFC 15 understood that unless the group acted in consensus with a shared understanding, the group could be thrown into conflict. The issue of welcoming new people into the group needed to be brought up and dealt with.

However, as is almost inevitable in a Small Christian Community, the members still find themselves in a dynamic tension about membership. Although they recognize the need to respect the dynamics of the group at any given time, they also remain committed to the ideal that Christians should always be as welcoming as Jesus was. So SFC 15 welcomes new members, dependent on the group setting priorities and on timing. Sometimes they have found it appropriate to close the community to newcomers. Temporarily. For instance, at a certain point after some members had left due to transfers, the community needed time together to process, grieve, pray, and to support and cherish one another.

Mostly, though, the doors to SFC 15 remain open and inviting to new members. Katie, one of the original members of the group, said: "I've realized the importance of planting seeds. I remember giving Susan a casual, off-the-cuff invitation at the grocery store. She started coming to our meetings, and came back to the church. It's in our brokenness that those seeds are planted, take root, and grow. I've learned that the invitation needs to be small, and with a follow-up. Sometimes the third or fourth offer will be accepted. You might accept out of guilt, but that doesn't mean the Holy Spirit isn't working within you."

Katie knows the power of invitation and finding community, too. "Frank called and asked me what I was doing on Wednesday night. I said, 'Nothing,' so he asked me to come to the Bible study group. I couldn't back out at that point. I was only going to come to one meeting, and then I was not coming again! That was eleven years ago. It was the end of something, but the beginning of me!"

Rolling Covenant

SFC 15 has developed three types of membership to deal creatively with the comings and goings due to business transfers: actives, associates, and former members. Actives are people who generally participate in the weekly gatherings. Associates have been members but are taking time out, or have shifted to ministries and activities in church that preclude their active participation in the small community. Former members have permanently left, usually because they have moved out of town. These types of membership work well and let people know that they are always welcome.

Another way of dealing with flux among members is what the group calls "rolling covenant." One community member explained how the rolling covenant works. "Every time we finish a block of material, or a new person joins us, we also ask ourselves how we're doing as a community. We spend time reflecting on what we want to do next and renewing our commitment to one another. The idea of a rolling covenant is a powerful way to remind people of the rules we use and of those things that are critically important in order for a group to remain bonded. At that time we also decide on the thrust of new material, an action, and a time frame. We make a commitment to one another for the time we work on that material. It prevents people from feeling trapped and provides new energy in the group." The rolling covenant helps the group stay open to new members, stay flexible in its expectations of active members, and review its priorities periodically.

SFC 15 knows that commitment may not last forever. At recommitment time people can comfortably leave for whatever reasons. Although leave-taking this way still requires a grieving process in the group, departing at the end of a commitment period is a healthy, graceful, respectful, and easy exit that allows closure for the group and for the person leaving.

For those who may have to leave because of a business transfer, the group half-jokingly tells them, "If you are thinking about leaving, you have to replace yourself before you go!" Carol noted: "That's helped everyone with the transition process. Nobody feels bad. It's harder when a person doesn't fit in well. We let them know that if they feel like they don't fit with the group, or if their values don't match with ours, they can go back to the contact person from the core team and request another group. Recognizing incompatibility is a sign of a healthy group and a healthy person."

Meeting

As in most Small Faith Communities, the structure of gatherings is simple and flexible. Members typically gather at someone's home, eat, pray, share the Good News from the Bible and from their life, and reflect together about their service to the larger community. For variety they organize special gatherings and sometimes focus their attention on burning issues that just have to be dealt with.

Carol has been a member of the community since it started twelve years ago. She recalls that the community started out doing Bible study using the Little Rock Scripture Series as the main focus of its meetings. When that ended, "we realized our affection for one another was growing, and that we needed something beyond that. We got connected with Fr. Art Baranowski, and moved to sharing our faith with one another. Our group has been growing ever since."

While the members of SFC 15 usually gather in one space for the prayers, they make musical chairs work for faith sharing. They have both big groups and small groups throughout the home where the meeting gathers. And as one member said, "In the groups, we also have an empty chair to represent and remind us of two things: that Christ is present as we meet, and that the stranger is always welcome."

When new people do come to a meeting, the community makes a conscious effort to help them feel comfortable. Instead of following the standard format, the community stops and discusses what it is doing. Everyone sits in a circle, and each member shares his or her story of work, kids, spouse, or close personal relationships.

Normally, though, faith sharing is done in groups of three or four because people find it easier to speak from their heart in smaller groups; they might be reticent in a group of eighteen. Said Katie: "That's really effective. Bill and I have been married for more than twenty years. He shared with me. But he began to learn to share more because he trusted that the group could be trusted. What astounded me was that he shared some things with the group before he shared them with me!"

When faith sharing ends, the community might come together as a whole for further sharing or for the closing prayer. Often the concluding prayer is a time of particular power. During this final prayer period, community members offer their petitions. Ann explained: "We have a prayer request book open during the meeting. Writing can be done by anyone, but usually before the meeting starts or after it ends. It's really neat for someone to notice, 'Hey, I prayed about that, and the prayer was answered!' Prayers do come true."

Besides the regular meetings, the community has Sunday brunch once a quarter, but any excuse is usually good enough for a party. "We've done game nights with kids included," said Katie, "where we had board games set up throughout the house and lots of snacks and goodies, of course. Recently a back-to-school party for the kids featured a Bible treasure hunt that Jacquie and Norma put together. Any given month has as many as seven birthdays or anniversaries for the community to celebrate."

The community helps members celebrate other special occasions, too. Carol recounted: "When Lawrence and I got married, after we planned the liturgy, the group did the rest. Everything! It was the most marvelous and touching thing anybody had ever done for me. It's the kind of thing that makes it okay for me to pick up the phone and call any of them anytime."

SFC 15 has a tradition of having a series of parties from Thanksgiving to Christmas. However, the week before Christmas is prayerful, calling everyone back to the real meaning of Christmas. Any visiting relatives are included in whatever the group is doing. Traditionally, the members take a group picture and send copies to all the former members as a greeting. Associate members are invited to all parties and special events. They do come.

Reaching Out

Membership in SFC 15 calls each member to service. How members serve depends on their gifts and circumstances. The community, children included, participates in at least one joint service project. Each Christmas they take part in Hope Center's program to sponsor a family who otherwise would have no Christmas. "One meeting is a wrapping party with the kids," said Katie. "Then, everyone who would like to gathers the next Saturday to deliver the gifts. We usually request one of the bigger families, because our Small Faith Community is so large and very, very generous."

For the most part, community membership draws each one to some individual service. For example, Carol's ministry is the community itself. She acts as facilitator. To do this task well, she has attended Buena Vista and NAPRC (National Alliance of Parishes Restructuring into Communities) national conferences for insights and information. She reviews resources for the community's use. Carol remarked: "This is my ministry. I was away from the church for fifteen years. When this group got started, I thought it was time to go back to church and fully participate."

Reflecting on his experience in SFC 15 and in the community he belongs to in his new parish, Bob felt it influenced his ministry in the workplace. First, the small community helped him deal with the pressure of being president of a service distribution company. He began viewing matters through a more Christian lens. This had some unexpected practical consequences. For one, he decided to hire a company chaplain for employees. "When I first took the idea to the company, a lot of people snickered. The chaplain's role is to be there to listen to the people. He helps people with emotional, financial, or marital situations, and also goes to the hospital to visit sick employees and their families, including when there is a new baby or a death. Recently an employee's son died after a long illness and the family asked the chaplain to say the funeral."

Personal Impact

Membership in the community has a personal impact on members that has been powerful and unexpected. Joella's story still inspires the community. On 9 December 1996, her doctor found a lump in her breast that had all the signs of cancer. She made an appointment with a surgeon. "I went home and told my husband that I didn't want to die, that I wanted to see my newborn grandson, Anakin, grow up." Two days later, on 11 December, Anakin died.

"With all the family worries during the funeral preparation, I didn't think about my health at all. Three weeks later I went to the surgeon, and the lump was no longer there at all. The dear Lord probably knew that I couldn't handle another tragedy. I truly believe that. I don't have family here. My Small Faith Community is family for me, and they were there, praying for and with me. I don't know what I would have done without them."

Katie provided a different perspective on the personal impact of the small community. "We all have friends, but until you have a spiritual connectedness with a friend, the relationship is limited. One time in our married life, my husband and I moved to Pennsylvania, where he is from. I knew that if life there got really tough, I could call the Edmond Small Faith Community, and they would be there for me. And it did get bad. On a night when I'd think that I couldn't cope anymore, I'd call them, or they'd call me. That's the Holy Spirit knowing the situation and responding. In Pennsylvania one day, my husband came home and said, 'It's time to move home.' We had no jobs and no money. We couldn't have done it without the Small Faith Community support. My daughter lived with Carol for a while and our son lived with a friend during the transition. When unrelated people bring suppers, unload furniture, and help with your kids, you know you are loved. Sometimes they put your needs before their own. That's the Holy Spirit responding."

New Challenges

Christ operating in a community draws more people to a group. Small Faith Community 15 recently reminisced about a cross-generational retreat it experienced. A ropes course was set up as an exercise in team building. It required that everyone rely on one another, stretch themselves to go beyond their usual capabilities, and solve problems. Given the physical boundaries of the first and second parts of the rope course, the instructor challenged them to work together to build a bridge between the two.

Community members were urged to push the parameters and yet maintain balance. Everybody had a role to play in the bridge building. When the task was completed, the instructor said of the group, "I have never seen a family group that did the kind of loving, caring, and sharing that you people did. I learned a lot."

SFC 15 now has a challenge ahead of it that will test both their ability to trust in one another and in divine providence, as well as its willingness to be open to new possibilities. The community realizes that it needs to consider a split, yet it wants to remain unified as church in its smallest unit. Over the years the number of members has increased. Their houses simply won't hold all the people.

"For one year we closed our doors as a community because about sixteen or eighteen people were coming every week," said Carol. "It was simply unwieldy. I suggested splitting the group into two, but the group gave a resounding 'No!' to that. Yet, if the groups are to reach their fullest potential, people always must have the idea to share their faith with more and more groups of people. One thing that happens in a Small Faith Community is that you become more confident about your faith and share it with others openly. It becomes evangelization in the best and most natural sense."

Another symptom of the need to split the group was that almost half of the members, for one valid reason or another, regularly declined preparing the prayers and content of the meetings. There were divisions also about focus. One half would rather focus on the social and prayer part of the gatherings. The other half wanted challenging content for sharing during the meetings.

So the community has been called to discern and acknowledge what the Holy Spirit is asking of it. In discerning the need for a split, Small Faith Community 15 is wrestling with the central question that has faith and invitation at its core: At what point do you have a Christian duty to reach out and invite other people to share faith with you? This process is ongoing and has not come to closure yet.

SFC 15 has challenges like any other group, but through long years of experience, it has learned to pinpoint problems and work through them together. The group members recognize that God has called them by name. Through prayer, sharing the Good News, community, and service, they are prophets in their own way. They are building, planting, and harvesting.

QUESTIONS FOR REFLECTION AND SHARING

1. Tell about a time when you were invited by name to something but didn't understand until much later what God was really inviting you to be or do.
2. Like Jeremiah 1:4–10, what barriers and protests are you inclined to put up when someone calls you forth?
3. The essential elements of church in its small community are prayer and ritual *(leitourgia)*, community *(koinonia)*, Gospel *(kerygma)*, and outreach in service *(diakonia)*. What does this community practice well? If you belong to a community, what balance does your community have of these four elements?
4. How do you feel about attempting to meet new parishioners and helping them to meet other people and become connected with your small community or another group in the parish?

5. What appeals to you about this group's sense of rolling covenants and three levels of membership: actives, associates, and former members? What problems might come from this sense of membership? What advantages?
6. As you read through this story, what did you find most memorable?
7. What is the Spirit asking of you through this story?
8. If your company president announced that a chaplain would be available to all employees, what would be your response?
9. What question is the Holy Spirit asking of you as a community? What is your response?

Loving God, we thank you for your presence here with us. Help us to be your presence for others by being better listeners or by taking a step forward in action instead of waiting for someone else to do it. Most of all, Holy Friend, help us to be church at home, at work, at school, or in the neighborhood. Inspire us to care about making the world a better place and to take actions to make it happen. Amen.

Moving from Group to Community

The Small Group of Large Faith
Edmond, Oklahoma

Living God, we welcome you in our midst and thank you for your presence with us. Help us to be open to your word through the Scriptures, story, and one another. Help us to cherish life as we cherish you. And help us, our God, to be a small group with very large faith.

The Good News from Matthew 13:31–32

> [Jesus] put before them another parable: "The kingdom of heaven is like a mustard seed that someone took and sowed in his field; it is the smallest of all the seeds, but when it has grown it is the greatest of shrubs and becomes a tree, so that the birds of the air come and make nests in its branches."

The Story of the Small Group of Large Faith

The Small Group of Large Faith belongs to the same parish as SFC 15, and, although connected to the parish and the other small communities, it has evolved in its own way. The same four elements of church permeate this community's life together, but take a shape unique to the people who form the Small Group of Large Faith.

"People used to ask us about our faith traditions," said Amy, "and I'd say, 'Ask my mother. I don't know why we do what we do as Catholics!' But now I am learning." As a cradle Catholic, Amy didn't feel strong in the faith until her husband, Brad, went through the RCIA program to become a Catholic. Then Carol, a friendly inviter from the parish's small faith community core team and a member of SFC 15 (profiled previously), came to the final class and encouraged them to continue with others as a small community. Amy and Brad got together with another couple and invited a group of people to meet with them. "But nobody came," said Amy, "so we decided to be the Small Group of Large Faith, as opposed to a large group with small faith. After a while the other couple had a baby, and it was very difficult for us to meet."

Two years ago, Amy and Brad decided to start again by sharing a Lenten experience with others from the parish. This Lenten experience has now evolved into a group of sixteen men and women, mostly in their thirties. Managers sit next to out-of-work folks, and everybody knows what ordinary is.

They see themselves as noisy, questioning, diverse, loyal, full of group wisdom and fun. "I think the laughter and jokes in the group are really important because it makes it real," said Christy. "We try to be as godly as we can, but I think our humanness comes out in the humor—especially when we laugh at ourselves."

One thing members bring to the community is trust. It's nice, they say, to be assured that what you say will remain confidential and not be spread beyond the group. That's one reason they consider themselves a healthy group: what's said in the group stays in the group. The cornerstone of their conduct rests on the premise that they respect one another's personal sharing and do not talk negatively about any members outside the group or even with someone else in the same group. This important principle was gently articulated at the beginning of the group's life together.

The exception to the rule is spoken kindness, compassion, love, and appreciation. Lynda put this in perspective, "We try to ask ourselves individually and as a group, 'Are we building up or tearing down?'"

Together, the Small Group of Large Faith has gone through marriages, divorces, breakups, births, and deaths of loved ones. Some are first-time experiences. They acknowledge that it's hard to find good Christian people to hang around with. Many haven't had a lot of friends because they want something more than a superficial relationship. Here, "all of us make it tick," said Matt. "It's a strategic fit because God is the strategist."

They are not only getting to know one another but are free to seek advice from one another. "We've only been married two years," said Christy, "and the group helps us by their experience." Matt affirmed that it works two ways: "It's really easy to give someone else advice, but when it comes to my own life, I'm like a numskull. I can't seem to practice what I preach. It's hard." And human. Said Brad, "It's very comforting to know others are going through the same things you are going through. We've all been tested in our faith, and this is the place where we affirm our faith."

Matt found the group's support immensely helpful when he was serving in Saudi Arabia after Desert Storm. "It was a real growing experience being away from family for ninety days. I kept thinking about what was going on back home, and realizing how quickly something could happen where I was. If there's anything to tell anybody about a small faith group, it's that it is not just about sharing your faith. It's about support in your life and about turning to one another in time of need, happiness, sadness, trials, tribulations, and blessings."

Goals of Formation

The Small Group of Large Faith meets weekly, year-round at Matt and Tiffany's home from 7:30 p.m. to 9:00 p.m. Why the group meets is clearly outlined in its written goals:

Short Term Goals:
>To begin and end on time
>To have monthly prayer partners
>To study the following areas:
>>History of the Mass/Order of Mass
>>Revelations
>>The Rosary, Mary
>>The Saints
>>The Seven Sacraments
>>Angels

Long Term Goals:
>   To integrate our faith life into our work life
>   To work as a small faith group on one community
>   service project per year
>   To become more knowledgeable about the Scriptures
>   To go through the catechism to learn more about the
>   Catholic church

Setting these goals serves three purposes for this group: focus, clarity, and preparation for a future that, for some members, includes educating children in the faith.

In addition to a group directory, each person has a three-month calendar with listings of topic, lesson, homework, leader, and food. The group members also have a short outline to remind them that listening, sharing, respecting, and thanking are essentials in their group process—not judging, debating, proving, or convincing. They understand that some groups don't necessarily need this structure, but they find it useful.

Meeting Format

After the usual socializing upon arrival, people settle down to spontaneous prayer that includes petitions for, for instance, a brother-in-law, someone in a car accident, guidance for families, someone's dad. One of the striking marks of this group is the deliberate and meditative way in which it makes the sign of the cross. It's slow and intentional. Then the members start reflecting together about the topic for that six-week block of time.

Among other things, they are now proud to know that there are twenty-seven books in the New Testament! Brad remarked: "I like to study things. In the Bible are real-life stories of people struggling with the same things we struggle with today. Except when we studied the Bible story of Daniel, we thought the world was going to end every day!"

Rotating facilitation empowers and strengthens the group to help it avoid overdependence on one or two people. In groups with only one facilitator, if that mainstay facilitator leaves, the group often flounders or falls apart.

Vital signs of life are omnipresent in the group as the members laugh loudly with relaxed freedom. Even in this generally lightsome group, lip biting, silence, and tears are mixed with sharing. And always they leave a chair empty, signifying Christ's presence.

As the evening closes, everyone kneels around the cocktail table for prayers of thanksgiving, the Lord's Prayer, and the Hail Mary. And for them, the sacred sign of the cross. "We live in the Bible Belt," said Lynda. "We try to practice Catholic traditions, like saying grace at meals whether we're in a restaurant or at home and blessing ourselves. We want to be identified as Catholic."

Crisis

The bombing of the Alfred P. Murrah federal office building in Oklahoma City, fifteen miles from Edmond, killed one hundred sixty-eight people, including seven people from Saint John's parish. One of those killed was a friend of community members Matt and Tiffany. They had just had dinner with him the Friday night before. Community member Brad called his wife, Amy, right after the blast shook his skyscraper. Amy, on the fifteenth floor of her eighteen-story building, confirmed that her building was shaking too. "Brad told me, 'It looks like Beirut here.' It didn't look like anything that could touch your community."

People reacted differently to these terrible events. But this event broke through everyone's defenses. As Lynda said, "When it's your mother and your child, reason leaves. Because of our faith and what we can bring to one another, we hold one another up from hopelessness."

Their small group had just formed. This crisis became a glue holding the group together. It bonded everyone in a swift shift from group to community. They needed one another's strength. "We wound up focused on the ability of Christ's love to bring everybody together after the bombing," remembered Randy. "The amount of love so far eclipsed the hatred that went into the bombing that it was overshadowed by the acts of goodness that followed."

"It was the innocent children that devastated us," said Lynda. "There was lots of confusion. We asked ourselves, 'Who did this?

Why? How could one human being do that to another?'" The group quickly put aside its six-week Lenten materials, and took two weeks just to talk about the bombing. "It opened up our whole group to being human and to sharing about themselves and God," said Amy. "It was a very intimate experience." Their group became part of groups huddled all over the country, holding on to one another in common vulnerability.

And the group members got mad at God. "The big question we asked," said Lynda, "was, How could God let something like that happen? The answer we finally came up with was that God didn't do it. He gives us free will to choose our actions." Believing helped the group come to its conclusion.

The community also took part in a public service of healing. Each person took river stone and marked their sins on it. Then they buried their sins beneath the marble marker for the Memorial Garden. It signified that they all wanted to give up their sinfulness. And it serves now as a continual reminder that all people are sinful, but that Christ offers redemption if they are willing to accept and live his message, his love. Community members also felt that the ritual and the memorial reminded them that acting in faith, hope, compassion, and love requires a daily choice. One of the community members concluded, "You can't go forward and grow if you are full of hate and negativity."

Outreach

What is clear to the Small Group of Large Faith is the ripple effect that a gathered small community living the tenets of Christ's love can carry into the larger world. "Sometimes, when we are so tired, we don't want to come to the meeting," said Amy, "but at some part of the meeting between the opening and closing prayers, something locked up inside of me can be released. We've all cried in this group, in sadness and in joy. We've cried because we have the Holy Spirit in our heart and we can release it. It comes from the Scripture verse, "'Love one another as I have loved you'"" (John 15:12).

"We invoke Jesus' name every time we gather," said Lynda. "Christ started out with twelve Apostles who started small communities. What we start here, we take out to the larger community."

All the group members give back to the larger community, whether with the Knights of Columbus, Rainbows (children who are grieving the loss of a loved one), youth ministry, confirmation programs, Promisekeepers, teaching, doing young adult ministry, or Christmas caroling at a nursing home. Randy mused: "We come together for nourishing our own spirituality, and having received that, we're able to go out to offer stewardship. You're better able to give from your abundance than from your need."

Impact on the Church and Society

"Now when I read the Scriptures for the day, certain people will come to mind," remarked Lynda. "What I've learned is that when I am thinking of them, I am praying for them. You can't make somebody hear what would be good for them. It only happens at the right time. But it does make a difference."

Brad continued: "We're committed to this way of being church because we're all trying to figure out how to bring God into the workplace a little bit more. I'm not sure I've figured that out yet. But it is a vocation. There is so much hate and anger and evil in the business world. I think about the early Christians and how they were attacked. When I come here, I can take what I need so I'm not as calloused when I go back to work and try to be humble. It helps."

One simple practice helps remind the members of their bonds and their commitment to serve one another. Every member has a prayer partner. Each member's name goes into a hat. They all draw the name of another member. For several days the prayer partner calls and shares a favorite Bible verse. Brad explained: "The person whose name I had was searching for wisdom at the time, so I tried to pick two verses that might be helpful to her. But my prayer partner forgot to call me! Later she did, though."

The parish has invited members to take part in its life as well. Amy remarked: "I was asked to sign up for an hour of eucharistic adoration. At first I said no because I work ten to twelve hours every day, and there are three thousand families in the parish who could participate. But then I said yes to every Friday at 6:00 a.m. It has been the most wonderful experience! I reflect, pray, do some journaling, then go to Mass. After that I go to work.

I keep it low-key, but a few people at work know. It makes a difference at work."

"One of the things I love about the Catholic church is its tradition," said Lynda. "It is based on community. That community has been present from the time of Jesus to the present through the Holy Spirit. It's based on unity, too. We have that to draw from. Just by the simple fact that we are trying to put that into our life, we become who we are. We don't have to tell people we are Catholic. Our actions will speak for us."

Wishes for Small Churches of the Future

When talking about the small churches of the future, Lynda's comment was typical: "My hope for the future of small faith-sharing communities as church? Get more started! Saint John's has had them for a long time. It's an opportunity for us to be there for one another and to build one another up. By doing that, we take it out to the workplace or wherever we are. It's very natural."

"My wish for the impact of SCCs is that we could have 90 percent of parishioners involved in a small faith-sharing community," said Amy. "Because I didn't feel my faith grow, or feel part of church, until I became part of this small community. I'd go to church and go through the motions, but I didn't feel the presence of the Holy Spirit in my life until I experienced the SFC setting."

"This has been one of the most fulfilling experiences of my life," said Randy. "In the last ten years, whatever has been offered by the church has all been accented on the small-faith-community style of how we deal with life. I feel very blessed to be with this group and look forward to being with the community for a long time."

QUESTIONS FOR REFLECTION AND SHARING

1. What touched you about the opening Scripture passage from Matthew, chapter 13?
2. What sticks in your mind about the story of the Small Group of Large Faith?
3. The bombing of the federal building hit this group hard. Has your group had any crisis to deal with? How was it both a challenge and an opportunity?
4. This community has several methods of staying focused: long-range and short-range goals, schedules, and so on. How can these methods be useful? What did you find appealing about this group's organization?
5. The members of this community felt that membership helped them to be more Christlike in their workplace. Would you agree that belonging to a small group has had or could have this effect on you? Try to explain your answer.
6. How does this group's story challenge you or your community to serve the larger community, to plant seeds of the Reign of God?
7. How does this community seem to be balancing the four essentials of church: prayer and ritual, Gospel, community, and service?
8. If the group is willing, put into a hat the names of each person in your small community and draw one name. Choose to pray for that person, to call him or her and share a Scripture verse, and to come to the next meeting to share what that experience was like.

Ever present God, you told us to love our enemies and to pray for those who persecute us. Jesus told us that you make the sun rise on the bad and the good and cause rain to fall on the just and the unjust. We join our prayers with the angels and saints, the great cloud of witnesses, for peace in our homes and communities. We raise our voices in prayer for all families who have lost loved ones because of violent, senseless acts. We ask your continued strength as we say, Our Father . . .

GRACEFUL FACILITATION

The Thursday Morning Group
Orange Park, Florida

Trustworthy God, we don't always trust you. Forgive our doubts about your provident care. May we let go of our need to control so that we can see, understand, and accept your constant, faithful love (Carol Schuck Scheiber, as quoted in *Open Hearts, Helping Hands,* p. 29).

THE GOOD NEWS FROM JOHN 13:1–16

Before the festival of the Passover, Jesus knew that his hour had come. . . . Having loved his own who were in the world, he loved them to the end. The devil had already put it into the heart of Judas son of Simon Iscariot to betray him. And during supper Jesus, knowing that . . . [he] was going to God, got up from the table, took off his outer robe, and tied a towel around himself. Then he poured water into a basin and began to wash the disciples' feet and to wipe them with the towel that was tied around him. He came to Simon Peter, who said to him, "Lord, are you going to wash my feet?" Jesus answered, "You do not know now what I am doing, but later you will understand." Peter said to him, "You will never wash my feet." Jesus answered, "Unless I wash you, you have no share with me." Simon Peter said to him, "Lord, not my feet only but also my hands and my head!" . . .

After he had washed their feet, had put on his robe, and had returned to the table, he said to them, "Do you know what I have done to you? You call me Teacher and

41

Lord—and you are right, for that is what I am. So, if I, your Lord and Teacher, have washed your feet, you also ought to wash one another's feet. For I have set you an example, that you also should do as I have done to you. Very truly, I tell you, servants are not greater than their master, nor are messengers greater than the one who sent them.

THE STORY OF THE THURSDAY MORNING GROUP

"Rose is a good facilitator of her Small Christian Community because she has the vision of the importance of those communities," said Roberta, on the staff of Saint Catherine's church in Orange Park, Florida. "She knows that the communities do not take away from church, but aid in bringing the community spirit to the larger parish. Rose is open and compassionate. She has had a diverse group over the last thirteen years. She's very welcoming, and she 'wears' her faith. You just feel it when you meet her.

"She does her homework, too," added Roberta. "If a papal document comes out, she researches it so she is an informed Catholic. Because of that, she's able to recognize an injustice and see it through to resolution. For example, when girl altar servers were not allowed, Rose went through all the right channels. First she approached the parish staff. Then she petitioned the bishop, and she persisted until approval was given." Rose will be seventy-three years old this year.

Who Are They?

In 1984, when a Renew program was implemented, Rose's group was called "Group 501." The first number signified the group number, for example, Sunday was group 1, Monday, group 2, and so forth. What the 01 meant was anybody's guess, but 5 stood for Thursday. Afterward, Group 501 became known just as a small group that meets on Thursday morning. Briefly the members considered naming themselves the Three Roses, referring to the three women of the same name (Rose W., the facilitator, and two Rose S.'s). But they were most comfortable with the Thursday Morning Group.

In the group are twelve women from sixty to eighty years old, and one man who attends with his wife. The parish priest was a member for five years until he moved to another parish. Initially, some of the members were not too excited about Father Peter joining the group. He gave great sermons, but they were not sure how he would do with faith sharing. "But it worked out really well," Billie declared. "He was fun! Down to earth! Human!"

Father Peter enhanced the group because he respected the facilitator's role and did not play "Who's in charge?" The group respected him and his extensive education in theology and canon law. Father Peter bridged the gap from pedestal to one-of-the-group by contributing wisdom from his own experiences, especially during times when the group was trying to make sense of difficulties. He and the group bridged the gap by being present one to the other. A priestly People of God does that for one another.

All but two of the group have retired-military spouses. Nearby Jacksonville Naval Base contributed to their choice of retirement location. "Our economic differences are not too great," said Rose, "although the incomes range according to rank, from enlisted to captain." With the exception of one native Floridian, everyone's children and grandchildren live out of state, from coast to coast.

The group members come from a generation in which a woman's identity came from her husband. Women's other gifts stayed hidden when their sole role was to marry, have children, and run the household. Most of the families moved all around the country. Community members reminisce about the time when cars were still a luxury and gas was eighteen cents a gallon. Ten cents bought a loaf of bread. A big bar of chocolate was five cents, and penny candy and ten-cent movies were the norms. Rose's husband's military pay was fifty dollars a week in 1947. Their first new car cost fifteen hundred dollars. The members of the Thursday Morning Group share a common understanding of how things used to be.

Sticking Together

Harmony reigns among the group. Georgia put it succinctly, "We really need one another for prayers, support, friendship, sharing—all those ingredients so necessary to fill the vacuum left by absent family members."

The group's members also recognize that all of them at different times make the group tick, and that Barbara certainly deserved recognition for her hospitality in letting them meet at her home over all the years.

Also, they have learned to trust one another and to trust in the promise of Christ that "'where two or three are gathered . . . , I am there among [you]'" (Matthew 18:20). Trust, not control, helped the group thrive. The parish wisely got the picture after they tried to set up a traditional core team for Small Christian Communities. "That didn't work here," said Roberta. "The people don't want that much structure. So we thought, 'Why fix something that's not broken!'"

Interdependency without suffocating the people by over-controlling is the guideline at Saint Catherine's parish. The parish encourages community members to meet for Advent and Lent and to stay in touch with one another in between. Small communities from one to thirteen years old are alive at Saint Catherine's. Some groups meet weekly, year-round.

The Thursday Morning Group is a seasonal small group with year-round socializing and involvement in the larger parish. A catechetical theme is used parishwide all year, even during the parish mission. This theme is followed by all the small groups through resources that are written by Roberta. As staff person for Small Christian Communities, she offers seasonal materials for the six weeks each of Advent and Lent. Included are facilitator guidelines, music, materials, and activities.

Roberta also offers training sessions three times a year for the facilitators, two on the parish level and one at the diocesan level. One of the guidelines helped Rose to get the idea right away. "Roberta said, 'Don't make it a Bible study course. Just help people understand the context and history of the times because it has such an impact on what is in the Scriptures.'" Two potluck dinners a year in the parish help the small communities to reaffirm their participation in the larger picture. So does a service project or two sponsored by the small-group program.

Rose takes several evenings to prepare for the small-group meeting. She gets well acquainted with the readings for the coming Sunday. A dictionary and biblical commentary are at her elbow so she can help the group understand the background and how the Scriptures fit with the times then. "The group really appreciates her, especially for helping us with that, because most of us don't have any background in Scripture studies. Rose has thirty years of being a catechist," said Billie.

Meeting Together

This community holds Jesus' promise that God is present when two or three gather as a foundational model for what it means to be in communion with one another. It also serves as a model for facilitation. Rose W., as the facilitator, is vivacious and funny. But perhaps what she does best is model what real group sharing is. Rose considers her role a privilege, but no big deal. While Rose takes pride in having been a catechist for over thirty years, she does not hang on to her role.

Her small-community friends have refused her many offers for someone else to share the facilitating of the meetings, but they do share the responsibility for group activities. Her facilitation empowers each person in the group to lead, to pray, and to love. Eleanor commented on this: "Usually you think of power in the secular sense. When we talk of the power of Christ, it has nothing to do with manipulation. Rose facilitates our knowledge of a loving power that touches us when we don't even know it. And it strengthens us when we call on him. When somebody is ill or depressed, Rose reminds us not to be afraid to pray to Jesus, and that his power will touch us. All we have to do is ask."

At the Thursday meetings, after the usual catching up with one another's life and lots of laughter, the people quiet to remember the presence of Jesus as the guest of honor. Spontaneous prayer or a prayer from the parish small-group booklet opens the gathering. Rose shares some information on the theme of the readings for the coming Sunday. Like any Christian welcomer, Rose draws others into the dialog during the meeting and encourages open-ended questions that help them to share in response.

One practice that the group especially likes is the African model for Scripture sharing. The Scripture message is read aloud. Then it is read again silently. People make note of a word or phrase that stands out in their mind, for example, fear. Then the group sharing explores what the word "fear" means for each one

at the moment or in the larger scope of life. Before the meeting ends, each person commits himself or herself to pray for a fear-free week for the person on his or her left. Everyone in the group prays for one another all week.

The Thursday Morning Group tries to say kind things about one another. The members support one another and grow through the good grace of one another's company. They have consistently accomplished over the years what many groups never can—they simply get along.

Moments of Grace, Ministering to One Another

The Thursday Morning Group has experienced many moments of grace. The most recent occurred just before Holy Week. It used John's account of the Last Supper, the only Gospel account that includes the story of the foot washing. Two of the Roses in the group washed the feet of the others with holy water from the Jordan River in Israel. The prayer service combined the Scriptures, hymns, and reflection on the meaning of the Eucharist as a call to serve our brothers and sisters. Everyone left feeling particularly refreshed and uplifted.

"That community ministers to one another," Roberta commented. They all looked after Theresa, who had the least of anyone in the group. They were painfully aware of the one small, drab room that Theresa called home. Brenda, her neighbor and friend, took Theresa out to dinner in local restaurants and drove her to the doctor's office. Gloria did Theresa's laundry, cleaned her room, and brought home-cooked meals. The Thursday Morning Group asked as a group, "Isn't this the true meaning of what church should be?"

Even the oldest of the group committed herself to service. Anna, a centenarian when she died, was a stalwart pioneer woman to whom idleness was a stranger. One day Theresa was caught dozing in the big chair during a community gathering. Anna, always the stoic, and sitting upright nearby, reached over with her cane and poked her twenty-three-years-younger friend, saying, "Wake up. Wake up!" Indeed, no breathing creature escaped Anna. On one of her frequent walks, she observed a family cat stretched out in a dead sleep. Applying her cane, she commanded in her thick German accent: "You sleep too much. Go chase the squirrels! Go do something!"

Failing eyesight didn't keep Anna from making twenty-five braided rugs for the small community's booth at the parish bazaar. She patiently took scraps that had been donated to the church, cut them into strips, rolled them tight, and eventually braided them. The proceeds help support a poor inner-city parish in Jacksonville. The deaths of her six-month-old daughter, a three-year-old son, and a son sacrificed to WWII, and thirty years of widowhood could not sap Anna's resolve. Making rugs was easy.

"We cannot comprehend how a Catholic small community can become navel gazers," said Rose. "That concept totally contradicts the Gospel message of who we are as Easter people." As such, community members make hospital visits, work in soup kitchens, collect money and goods for a Haitian project, and drive disabled neighbors to the store or just out for a ride.

Christmas Pain

The group members associate many Scripture passages with their community. For Rose, the image that comes to mind in the life of the community during Christmas 1995 was Lazarus, representing rebirth and resurrection.

Anna drew her last breath on 23 December. She had fought the good fight for all her one hundred and two years. Even with Christmas approaching, no one was sad for Anna, who was celebrating the achievement of her last goal: celestial solace.

However, the Christmas Day suicide of Rose S.'s youngest son shocked the group members to the core. "Joe gave us no indication that something was wrong," cried Rose. "I called to invite him to join me for Christmas Eve Mass. He said, 'No, I'll see you tomorrow.'" When Rose got home from Mass on Christmas Day, the awful news sank in. Her thirty-four-year-old son had shot himself with his own shotgun.

Joe had a diving accident at age twenty-nine. Everyone thought that he had made a remarkable adjustment to living as a paraplegic. He had his own apartment, went to the grocery store by himself, did his own laundry. Looking back though, Rose wondered if seeing his friends marry didn't make Joe feel terribly alone. "Just the week before, he asked me if he could move back in with me, and I told him, 'Sure. Let's plan it out.'"

On 26 December, Rose W. had made most of the necessary phone calls to the group about Joe's death. Two days later she came home from the grocery store to find her husband, Sam, waiting for her at the door. "Jennifer was killed in an auto accident," he said. Their fifteen-year-old granddaughter was gone. Rose fell to the kitchen floor, repeating over and over, "Oh God, no, no, no!" The next days were a blur for her. Billie took over making the phone calls that Rose had so many times made for everyone else.

At the memorial service and reception for Joe, the community clung together and held one another up. For his mother, Rose S., the suicide itself caused terrible pain, but not having a chance to say good-bye made it even harder. "When you can look at your son in a coffin, you can say good-bye. But I couldn't do that because Joe was cremated. I really felt cheated."

Today Rose S. is understandably still grieving, but moving toward peace. "God has given me the strength, love, and mercy to go on," said Rose. "If I wasn't in a relationship with the Lord, or in a small group, I just don't know where I'd be today. I think the Lord was preparing me for this. I was a hospice volunteer for ten years. I've been through a lot of grieving periods with people who have lost loved ones. I just thank God for giving me my son for thirty-four years," she continued. "He was just on loan. They're all God's children." Rose W. also credits the outpouring of love from her small community and parish with getting her through the tragedy of her granddaughter's death.

One of the particularly striking characteristics of this group is its sensitivity to one another's needs. The members made a special effort to talk at length on the phone with those who were out of town when the deaths took place. They seemed to understand that closure in those relationships would be hard when the absent members returned, not having had the rituals of wake, funeral, or memorial service to help them process their grief.

Transformations

Even though all the group members had experienced many losses over the years, the Christmas deaths changed each of them. No one plans a week like that one. Fortunately, the process of coming together regularly in fellowship, prayer, sharing, support, and service had changed them too. They had all become more compassionate, less judgmental. Billie said: "You can spend years with people in a group and never really know them. When these deaths happened, we began to share at a down-deep level. As I listened I began to understand them differently. It made me sit back and admire them. The whole small community experience has been a real eye-opener. I've learned to listen better, and I've enjoyed it thoroughly."

Dolly and Georgia have recently come into the group and are blending in well. Even so, Dolly was not prepared for the impact Jesus could make in a group. "At first, I couldn't speak because I could feel a sense of God's presence that placed me on the verge of tears."

Georgia had stayed outside the church for thirty years. During a major crisis in her life, the power of a simple invitation brought her back. She wouldn't have made the move herself, because she didn't know if she would be welcomed or accepted. The Thursday Morning Group brought her spirituality to life amid loving friends. Now Georgia has been able to own the grace to forgive and to mend some fences.

Theresa died in March. The group can imagine her laughing with Jennifer, Joe, and Anna—and sending blessings on the Thursday Morning Group.

QUESTIONS FOR REFLECTION AND SHARING

1. What touched you from the Scripture reading? What word stays with you?
2. What touched you from the Thursday Morning Group's story?
3. Who do you most relate to in the Scripture reading or in the community story? Why?
4. The group had some reluctance about Father Peter's membership. How did you feel about this? What made it possible for them to overcome their concerns?
5. What sort of ritual could a Small Faith Community use that would have the same meaning as Christ washing the Apostles' feet? Would such a ritual enhance the solidarity of your community? If yes, how?
6. Of the four essentials of church, what stands out in this story?
7. Billie's favorite Scripture passage is Philippians 4:13: "I can do all things through him who strengthens me." Tell about a time when you felt that strength.
8. What one small step will you take to be a better foot washer?

Brother Jesus, thank you for a comforting word. Keep close to me. I don't ask to see the distant future; one step at a time is enough for me. But one thing I do ask. Let me feel your hand, let me hear your gentle voice, and lead me on. Amen (David Suley, as quoted in Koch and Culligan, comps., *Open Hearts, Helping Hands,* p. 32).

Neighborly Love, Family Style

**Saint Martin DePorres Small Christian Communities
New Haven, Connecticut**

Holy Friend, teach us the virtue of acceptance, which means "to receive willingly." You give us grace to give. Now we ask for grace to learn acceptance (Dagmar Arango, as quoted in *Open Hearts, Helping Hands,* p. 25).

The Good News from Luke 10:25–28

A lawyer stood up to test Jesus. "Teacher," he said, "what must I do to inherit eternal life?" He said to him, "What is written in the law? What do you read there?" He answered, "You shall love the Lord your God with all your heart, and with all your soul, and with all your strength, and with all your mind; and your neighbor as yourself." And he said to him, "You have given the right answer; do this, and you will live."

The Story of Saint Martin DePorres Small Christian Communities

Four Small Christian Communities are represented in Gertrude's living room. The portrait of the Last Supper above the sofa seems right and natural with black Apostles and a black Christ. "We are Catholics first. Then we're Black Catholics," said Gert. "We come from different regions of the world, and yet we have the same philosophy and wish in life to serve our Lord and Savior."

The group in her living room pays attention as she offers the opening prayer for their meeting: "Lord, once again we gather, and give all glory, honor, and praise to you and to your son, Lord Jesus Christ. Lord, there is a mixture of groups here tonight, and we ask that you join us, and we thank you for everything that you have put before us, and we thank you for everything that you will put before us. We ask, dear Lord, that you bless those who are not with us tonight, and allow them in some way to know that we are thinking about them. Lord, we ask that you join each and every one of us and that your spirit goes deep into our heart so that we can show one another how much we love one another and how much we love you. In the name of your son, Jesus, we pray. Amen."

This is a typical beginning for the handful of Small Christian Communities at Saint Martin DePorres Church in New Haven, Connecticut. They formed three years ago because many parishioners wanted an avenue for friendship, and something more than Sunday liturgy. At the beginning the searchers needed someone to lead them.

Father Elko, the pastor, suggested Sr. Joan Bernier. When Joan met with the group, she discovered that the people had not come to learn about organizing small groups. They wanted her to lead the small groups. None of the parishioners felt that they could do it. Sister Joan respectfully declined, telling them that they had to take the lead. That was her gift to them.

The people in Saint Martin's small communities agree that they all make the SCCs tick by sharing responsibility. But Gert got them going and took ownership from the beginning. She called Sister Joan and asked her to please come back. "You come and train us, and we'll go forward with it and be responsible." In six weeks Joan taught ten people how to facilitate small communities. "It was a powerful group," Joan recalls. "They were very involved with prayer. The faith sharing was at a very deep level."

After that training experience, the facilitators were excited and wanted to share what they had learned with the larger parish of three hundred and eighty families. They composed a questionnaire that asked people if they wanted something more in their life. Agnes gave a homily at every Mass. "The church was always packed," Joan remembers. "Agnes was inspiring. She basically said to the people, 'This is what happens in a Small Christian Community. We want you to be involved.' There was never a better black preacher. Then, Father Elko walked up and down the aisles of the church and said: 'I want this parish to be small communities. These people are trained. They know what to do.'"

Many Communities, One Unit

These small communities at Saint Martin's are one unit. It's hard to tell where one group leaves off and another begins, and they are all closely connected to the parish. Gert remarked: "Even though we were separated in little households all over the city, SCC brought us all together in sharing. It's made us closer to people at church. To be involved with one another and to share our lives in all the trials, tribulations, and sadnesses as well as the joys is one of the most important things that God wants us to do."

"When you form SCCs in the parish," said Joan, "something happens to the parish. People greet, hug, kiss, talk. There is real joy. It's a joyous noise unto the Lord. And in a black community," she continued, "the choir waltzes down the aisle with their robes flowing. The music is spectacular. The priest is dancing with them. It's a total celebration with their hearts and souls in it. Sunday morning is not for private prayer. It's for communal celebration. Here, it's an Alleluia from head to toe."

Agnes defined what makes the difference in the style of spiritual worship in her parish. "Speaking as an African American, it has a lot to do with our roots. At some point in our growing-up life, we experienced people putting their hands up and freely showing their enthusiasm, especially in worship. Hispanics, Latin Americans—all the cultures bring music from their heritage. Praising the Lord comes from our heritage. If we want to say "Amen, Alleluia," we do. And when Father Elko is preaching, it gives him some idea that we're listening. You have to let go and let God have his way. You can't hold back, the Spirit is trying to work in you. Don't worry about what people think or what you look like. You miss your blessing by holding back. You miss out on the joy."

Coming Together

The groups meet weekly, bimonthly, or monthly, but take the summers off. They have grown to depend on one another, and the frequency of gathering is directly related. A weekly or bimonthly meeting enables greater growth than a monthly meeting. Much happens in one month, and if a person misses one meeting, two months pass before the next gathering.

For some, the weekly meeting is mandatory. They simply have to keep in touch. Gert tells of one instance when she called Fred, a member of her group. He reported that he wasn't feeling well. That worried her and the other group members. They canceled their meeting and some members went to Fred's house. They found that he was having a stroke. Gert said: "We got him to the hospital just in time. If we hadn't met every week, I don't want to think what would have happened to our dear friend Fred. If we don't have a meeting, we make sure we check with Fred to see how he is doing. He's doing fine now." The people in the groups have grown to miss one another if too much time goes by between meetings.

At the meetings, groups have different approaches. However, like Small Christian Communities throughout the world, all the groups pray together, read and talk about biblical passages, share their recent experiences of faith, and conclude with more prayer. How all this is done varies. For instance, in one community Agnes is good at setting the environment with flowers, the crucifix, the Bible, and at helping people to follow Quest, their resource. Linda values the liturgical times, and her group focuses on seasonal themes like the coming of Jesus or Christ's Passion.

Gert's group doesn't use just one resource all the time. It concentrates on a mix of the Scriptures and theology because a group member has a theology background and is excellent in helping the community to see through that lens.

"Whatever the inclination of the group," Earl explained, "Small Christian Community is a good learning tool. It brings people together in a very effective way to get to know more about the Bible, our religion, and our relationship with Christ on a daily basis as it connects with the Scriptures. This kind of church is like Thanksgiving. You eat, sing, and pray together."

Members of Saint Martin's groups agree that studying and praying with the Bible has been a big change from their religious education as children. Rather than learning rote answers to the catechism, they now read the Gospels, study them, and try to take them to heart.

Even a bitter Connecticut winter could not prevent Linda's SCC from meeting. She recalled: "The weather had been bad for some time and none of us could get out of our house. Because our meetings are the pause that refreshes, we set up a conference call with six people on the line. I was upstairs in my mother's room sitting in the dark. We really felt connected, especially because we had to listen intensely. Without seeing one another, we knew who was talking. It lifted our spirits so very much. The joy is seeing Jesus in other people. I'll never forget it."

When members have to miss meetings, they feel comforted because they know that the others are lifting them up in prayer. They know that they will get through trials because they are being prayed for. They have witnessed the power of God answering prayer and carrying them on the daily journey. "Small Christian Community makes us church for one another," said Maxine, "and makes us aware that we should be church for others outside the group. It makes the word of God come alive. Then we add our story to it and bring that forth into the world to share."

Pastor and People, Perfect Together

At Saint Martin DePorres, the Small Christian Communities and the pastor form a close partnership. Rather than stifling or intruding into the life of these communities, the pastor, Father Elko, works closely with them. "Father Elko was wise," said Agnes. "Rather than coming in and changing everything, being in charge, he just said, 'Show me what you're doing.' He is a very good preacher because he will reflect on something that's personal in relationship to the Gospel. He's down to earth, and makes his homily something people can relate to in the context of both his struggles and yours. And when he gets into it, he gets up on his toes, and we know he's caught up in the Spirit."

"I was in a Maryknoll missionary program years ago," said Father Elko. "I had read about Small Christian Communities in third world countries. Real Gospel values emerge from anyone that is oppressed. One of the reasons that small community works here is that the word comes alive. The Gospels speak to oppression and poverty. African Americans have always had to live with oppression. Their faith is very real because of all the mess they have had to put up with.

"I see the Gospel spirit here in the parish. You can't explain it. You just have to experience it. The word and the people feed off of one another, and the power is enormous. You see and feel the living word. It's easier to preach because what I say resonates with them, and they respond right before my eyes."

The pastor has a lot to say about the tone in his parish. Father Elko's tone is harmony through inclusion, and the bylaw is baptism. "We're all called to be priests and ministers of one another in shared responsibility. I decided I was not the all-knowing leader. The person leading the parish is the Holy Spirit. The master is Christ, and all of us are to participate in discerning the will and direction we are being called to follow. Everyone has gifts. No gift is superior. No title is dominant. And titles are not turf."

Another way this pastor sets the tone and the example of service for the small communities and the parish is by tutoring children in the public schools in math, reading, or anything the teacher says the children need help with. Father Elko tutors in the mornings unless he has a funeral. "I strongly believe that someone from the church should be present in the kids' lives. Church shouldn't be just a church building sort of thing. In a talk she gave to the bishops just before she died, Sr. Thea Bowman, a black woman celebrated for her spirituality, said, 'The most important thing you can do for us is education.' That's one reason I am involved in the public schools nearby."

People on a Mission

Evangelization and outreach in service are ingrained in these small communities. Linda explained: "SCC has helped me with my spiritual development, filled for me a need to look at how God is moving in my life, and helped me to listen and to do things and to not be afraid. You try to be a better Christian!"

The Saint Martin DePorres Gospel choir has become the primary means of evangelization for members of the communities. It lifts up the name of Jesus in jails, Catholic and Protestant congregations, and many other places throughout the area. It offers a rich mixture of Gospel music sung by a Roman Catholic, African American church choir. Being in the choir has been a great outreach for people of the city, but has also been inspirational and joyful for the members, too.

This effort by the choir is also matched by the good works of many individuals in the parish. Butch, a policeman in a public school, is a good example of how the small community and the parish draw people to be better Christians. One evening during a facilitators' meeting, Butch apologized to Sister Joan for being so tired. He had been at the church since 5:00 a.m. cooking the meal for a funeral, then going to the Mass and the cemetery, serving the meal afterward, and staying to clean up.

The Spirit among the people calls them to do everything they can for one another. The celebration after Sunday Mass can go on for an hour and a half or more, with bacon and eggs for breakfast. Sister Joan declared: "They leave when the Spirit suggests. They don't rush out of the parking lot, cutting one another off."

A member of another group, Maxine, is called Mary Sunshine by her small community. Even though she serves the community as a visiting nurse, her other ministry is giving hugs. She shared one thousand hugs last year. The hugging started when Maxine realized through the Small Christian Community process that she might not be an organizer or activist, but she could hug folks who needed it.

Gert, retired from a career at the telephone company, is the mother of two, grandmother of four, and foster parent to several more children. About all the children that she loves, clothes, feeds, and guides through life, she said: "I don't have anything to do with it. Whenever I try to deviate from that, it never works out. So it's the Lord's plan for me to take care of all these children. I believe in God. I talk to God constantly. It keeps me sane and keeps me going. I am never alone. I know that God is there listening and helping me along."

"All Small Christian Community experience helps you do your job better because you care more, like 'This is my giving.

This is my love,'" Agnes explains. "People would just as soon step over you as talk to you in this world. We are tempted to act in ways at work, home, and school that are real, but not really Christian. So we also have to do like it says in Ephesians 6:11 and 'put on the whole armor of God, so that [we] may be able to stand against the wiles of the devil.' We have to be ready so the devil will not influence our thoughts and our behavior. SCC makes you want to do more for your neighbor and to do things as Christ did them. If you see a homeless person on the street asking for a dime, you don't have to give all your money away, but SCC has helped us to learn how to reach out to one another and be shelter for one another. We ask people who are homeless in the street what their name is, and we bring that person by name to the prayer petitions. We do not begin or end our choir rehearsals without prayer."

Columbus House is a center for homeless people. Small community members often help out there. Gert described the good that the community members do and the gifts that are given back: "Clients loved to see us come there. We could never understand why. It wasn't necessarily because of the food we were preparing for them. It was our interaction with them. They really enjoyed our company. When I realized that they enjoyed our company, it gave me a sense of, 'Well, I've reached another little plateau here,' because I'm not seeing people differently anymore. I try to stress that now to my grandchildren. You must meet and greet everyone the same way, because you never know when you are looking into the face of Jesus. Never. Ever. I've definitely grown in that area." Gina agreed: "The people see that we put a little love in the food, and I think that's important. It fits with the interaction. When somebody takes a piece of chicken, washes it, cleans it, seasons it well, prepares it, and serves it with a smile, that makes a whole lot of difference."

The group's outreach is not limited to the local community. Saint Martin DePorres parish twins with a parish in Haiti. Linda recalled: "Because of our mission to that parish, we need to be spiritually anchored and operate as a Small Christian Community, not just as a parish committee. We wanted a human connection from family to family, not just give a donation but be a partnership. It's a mutually enriching relationship within the One Body of Jesus."

Butch, Gina, Earl, Linda, Edith, Jim, Maxine, and Gert are stories in the Living Word. Their story and the stories of the other
members of Saint Martin's Small Faith Communities may be easy
to miss. They seem like ordinary people in the soup kitchen. Or
when singing in the Gospel choir that goes all over Connecticut
joyfully bringing the word to others. Or when one of them takes a
younger woman under his or her wing. Or when a small, elderly
woman gets groceries for her neighbor every day. But the story is
alive among the small communities of Saint Martin DePorres parish.

QUESTIONS FOR REFLECTION AND SHARING

1. What part does prayer play in this community? in your life?
2. Share your thoughts and feelings about this statement: One
   way you can tell if you are praying enough is that you get
   along better with your neighbor.
3. List words that describe your neighborhood.
4. What words would you like to have describe your relationship with your neighbors?
5. How does the pastor of Saint Martin's make blooming Small
   Christian Communities possible in the parish?
6. Was Sister Joan right when she told them that they had to
   take the lead? What makes people think that they cannot take
   the lead?
7. The facilitators of the groups visit one another's groups. Why
   would this be a rich experience?
8. How do these Small Christian Communities build God's
   Reign? Share ways you are a good steward of God's bounty.
9. Of the four essentials of church, what seems to shine about
   these small communities?
10. What is your experience of parishes welcoming diversity and
    variety? How can SCCs welcome more diversity? How would
    they benefit?

*Forgiving God, Jesus loved an open and accepting spirit. You ac-
cept us just as we are. Teach us to accept other people for who they
are. May we learn from one another and love one another. Amen*
(Koch and Culligan, comps., *Open Hearts, Helping Hands*, p. 28).

Rites of Passage

The Faith Family Small Church Community
Denver, Colorado

Loving Creator, every day is a passage from the day before. Help us to listen today with open hearts to hear what you want us to hear. Help us to value each person's story as a reflection of your story. We place before you now the people who are not able to be with us and ask your blessing on them.

The Good News from Psalm 118:21–24

> I thank you for having heard me;
> you have been my savior.
> The stone rejected by the builders
> has become the cornerstone;
> this is Yahweh's doing,
> and it is marvelous to see.

The Story of the Faith Family Small Church Community

The Faith Family Small Church Community had been invited to join the other small communities from the parish for a retreat. The Faith Family community eagerly anticipated this time away because the members imagined relaxation, laughter, meditation, quiet conversation with God, and peace.

By the morning of the third day, peace had become a dream. The turmoil had started with an innocent question posed by the retreat team: "What keeps you from sharing more deeply with your community?" It was clearly an invitation for the community

61

members to take off the masks of polite superficiality. The communities were encouraged to spend the rest of the evening sharing. But this group's sharing became more like a nightmare.

This parish-based small community was almost two years old. Its members were friends. At least they thought so. Ordinary people living ordinary lives: Barb, Bill, Ed, Joy, Ellen, her husband Terrance, and the rest of the members. They were a sampling of human diversity, and they thought they were a community. The retreat had been going so well. Now they were in a mess. Confused, dazed, and in shock, group members took shots at others in the group. What went wrong?

The Powder Keg

Several ingredients for trouble had been brewing for a while within the group, but members were not aware of the rising tension. When the group was forming, it had had a minor tug-of-war over what the group would be about. Allen had been to Medjegoria and wanted it to become a prayer group, saying the rosary at every meeting. The group members agreed that while the rosary was an excellent idea, they wanted a larger view. It was a polite way to say "No way!" to Allen's idea.

The second ingredient to the rise in tension took place when Allen suggested that they have a clothing collection for needy Bosnian children. Everyone thought this idea was great. They could all help. It would be simple. Joy thought probably a pickup truck and a horse trailer would do the job. And Joy's word was Gospel in the community.

The clothing project got out of hand quickly, but the community members felt that they had to proceed because they had consented to the project from the beginning. Of course, going along with the idea was not the same as taking full ownership. Allen had asked for donations on television. Viewers were affected. A little girl brought her favorite doll to send. A woman came with a one thousand dollar check and said, "I have nothing to give but this." Clothes became mountains and had to be sent to another parish for sorting. Soon the community had to use semi-trailers to hold the donations, which still had to be sent overseas. When the clothes were on their way to Bosnia, the group felt happy, tired, . . . and used.

The third source of tension occurred soon after the second one. Three men in the group were all in the same car on the way to a gathering. To his captive audience, Lester said that he was gay. Allen replied, in no uncertain terms, that it was wrong and that the church teachings quite clearly condemned homosexuality. Clearly, Allen declared, Lester was going the wrong way on a one-way street. The men's strong personalities were heading them and the community on a collision course.

When the group members all went on the retreat together, at least four key factors were at play:

1. They had no idea that the group tension level was so high.
2. They had new and old resentments all bunched up together.
3. No process was in place to help them uncover tension, name the issues, and deal with them in some kind of reconciliation process.
4. On top of all that, they had high expectations for a relaxing retreat with good friends.

On retreat, the community started coming apart.

Allen and Bill, the sternly conservative, hard-line Catholics, were on the firing line. The group turned against them and said that they were acting "holier than thou." Conversation grew intense and blunt. All faces turned to Ellen, the facilitator, who had moved physically further and further away from the group. She said nothing.

Then a change happened. One by one, people began telling their stories, moving away from issues and into personal reflection. Even though the tension was still hard to handle, eventually they began trying to make sense of the experience that would in time become a classic story of their community. Recalling this moment of crisis and opportunity, Ellen, the facilitator, said: "The interesting thing about that evening was that we were honest about who each of us was individually. We shared a lot of our pain, and we really hadn't done that up to then. There was anger, but that was okay. We got through it."

The night's session was immensely difficult. Tempers got out of hand. Raw feelings got exposed. The group members went to bed wondering if any of the others would show up for breakfast. Or if they would still be talking to one another.

Everyone came to breakfast and eventually conversations started. The explosion had broken down barriers, and the sharing had started building bridges between the members. Ellen confessed: "We all kind of realized our humanness. But it was really hard. I'll never forget the look on Bill's face when people were challenging him, like, 'Ellen, you're the facilitator. Help me! Aren't you going to do something?' But I didn't know what to do! I was not sure where it was supposed to go, and I don't like conflict either. I was scared to death."

The community members prayed and tried to trust that God would help them grow through this upheaval. They found reassurance with their pastor, and the closing Mass brought them together for healing. Even so, Ellen added: "It took us a long time to trust one another enough to talk openly about it. The healing was slow."

After the retreat Allen left the group in search of a prayer group that would meet his needs for the rosary and meditation. The members of this Small Church Community learned experientially what they already knew in their heads: all religion is relational. And that implies something beyond the beginning stage of politeness.

Now, uncertain of how it was supposed to be, the group members asked themselves individually, and often, "What was that all about?" until they had answers about themselves and the group. Ed recalls: "Before that retreat weekend, everyone shared superficially. The retreat made us risk. We shared our heart and soul. After that we knew what made people tick, what made them feel good, and what hurt them. So sharing was at a different level after that, both as a listener and as one who shares. We opened up and became vulnerable. I think we became open to the Lord, too. God helped us to set the mold for our group."

The Glue

The community works hard now to communicate well. But the process to open sharing was slow and personal. With a chuckle, Bill remembered, "I was debating a lot whether I was being asked to leave!"

"And I give Bill a lot of credit for staying," said his wife, Ann. "Each week, I'd ask him, 'Do you want to go to the small church meeting?' It went back and forth between us in discussion privately, and we talked a lot of things out. But at the beginning I wondered, God, why is this happening to our group? Especially when I felt it was going to fall apart. Then there was that scary part of, well, you know, how are we going to get through it?"

The group realized that sometimes it would have to seek outside help to work through its issues, but it persevered. Most of the community acknowledge that the grace of perseverance is the glue that keeps it going. Sue remembered: "We all wanted it to work, so we stuck it out. Even though it was hard for us, we kept coming back for more! With outside help, somehow we survived and got stronger as a group."

Celebration

Another kind of glue that has held this group together during rough times was the celebrations before and after that infamous retreat. Ann and Bill were dating when they became part of the Small Church Community. The small-community process helped them decide whether they wanted to deepen their relationship. When they decided to marry, the community helped plan the wedding.

This seven-year-old community calls itself the Faith Family Small Church Community. Gathering twice a month, the members first catch up with one another's life, eat together, then light the Faith Family candle. The more structured part of the meeting follows the candlelighting and focuses on sharing the Scriptures and offering prayer requests.

Invitations

Over the years, the Faith Family community has made inviting people into the community and into Christian life a key part of its ministry. Joy demonstrates creative invitations at work. She has invited coworkers on either side of her to say the rosary while they pack crackers so often that they know how many boxes they can pack to ten Hail Mary's, an Our Father, and a Glory Be to God.

Indeed, Sue's membership in the community started when Ellen invited her and her husband, Ed, to go to church. Ellen laughingly said to them, "Just thought I'd ask. You can go to the noon Mass. You can even sleep in and still make it!"

Sue and Ed had attended Protestant congregations. In fact, she grew up in them, and her grandfather and many of her uncles were ministers. But she and Ed did not feel at home in the Baptist, Methodist, and Pentecostal churches they had visited. They never even considered the possibility of the Catholic church. When Ellen invited them to church, they decided to try it.

"We liked it," said Ed. "We felt welcomed. During the Lord's Prayer we held hands, and it was powerful. I wanted to come back because I felt spiritually fed. We just kept coming, but didn't go to Communion because we didn't know what the beliefs were. It was a good thing we didn't go because it encouraged us to find out."

From this invitation Sue and Ed eventually began the Inquiry program and finally started the RCIA (Rite of Christian Initiation of Adults, also known as the catechumenate). At this point Ellen invited them to a small-community gathering. Again, the invitation came at the right moment. Sue and Ed liked the group and realized that it fit a need in them. Sue recalled: "Throughout the RCIA process, we found small community really helpful because there are so many things you want to learn. With all the different people, I was encouraged about how they lived their faith, what they heard in the Scriptures. That was really valuable because it helped me to sort things out."

Converting, One Day at a Time

While the invitation to small community helped Ed and Sue, they now needed the help of the community for the next phase of their spiritual journey. They felt excluded because they could not take Communion even though they believed. Then came another blow to Sue and Ed. One of the community members commented, "It was hard for the whole small community because Sue and Ed felt a sense of rejection when they were told they couldn't continue with RCIA until they had their previous marriages annulled."

After considerable praying and discernment with the community, Sue and Ed decided to proceed with the annulment process. Both of them dreaded having to dredge up old hurts that they had left behind years before. They had to find witnesses and get their help.

"All of us were angry," Ellen remembered, "that they had to
go through that. We'd go to noon Mass together and then go out
to breakfast. Those meals together as a community were terribly
important to answer their questions, especially because of the
anger in all of us. And we needed to share that at table together. Here were people obviously wanting to become Catholic. And
we saw how important the Eucharist was for them. Like in the
Scriptures, their hearts were really burning with longing for it. It
seemed so wrong that man-made rules got in the way. Many of us
said, 'Christ wouldn't have done this.' We all had to work through
quite a few things in that period of time while their annulments
were in process." So the annulment process had a plus side for
members of the community. They had to ask tough questions
about their relationship to the church and discern a Christlike response.

The community proved indispensable for Ed and Sue. "Because the annulment process was so hard, if it hadn't been for our
Small Church Community, we would have left. The rejection we
felt was so bad. But being supported by the people gave us the
strength. As I look back now, as tough as it was, I shared a lot
more. Maybe I wouldn't have learned as much either."

The annulment process took four years from the time Ed
and Sue started the RCIA process. Finally, at Easter Vigil, the two
were received into the church, and the community was present.
When their marriage was blessed, the community was there. And,
Sue added, "God was in the arms of it all."

Another surprise came into play through the process, too.
The "come and see" invitation had a ripple effect. Barb had been
born and raised Catholic. Religiously going to Mass on Sundays
and holy days, she fulfilled her duty, but it didn't fulfill her. As an
admittedly shy person, she had still felt like a stranger in the
church. She did know Sue and Ed. After they started attending
church, they invited Barb to go along. Then they invited her to go
with them to their small church gathering. Barb remarked, "It was
really neat the way they accepted me right from the beginning,
even though I didn't talk much."

Besides feeling welcomed by the community, Barb began
learning new things about the church she had attended all her
life. "I was still going on grade school information like, 'You can't

go to a different church—even with a friend.' I was afraid to explore it all until Sue and Ed wanted to continue on with the catechumenate and asked me to be their sponsor."

Now Barb became even more excited about her faith. She even has been discerning whether to seek an annulment of her marriage. "My faith life is much richer and more connected. I know I have the support from my Faith Family Small Church Community during the process."

Caregiving

The community has been of service in various ways since the clothing drive for war victims in Bosnia. However, the true spirit of service came out in their caregiving to Lester.

At the time of the retreat, he had been diagnosed as HIV positive. Eventually he had full-blown AIDS. Lester declared: "The Faith Family is my family. They help me to live life, not death. It calms me. The message they give me is, 'We'll be here for you.' And they are, especially on the days when I can't get out of bed because I am immobilized. They have a phone chain. If one can't help, another does. They get medicines and groceries for me. They sit with me, pray with me. In many aspects I feel unworthy to walk the path with this community because I think they're holy.

"When you are terminally ill," said Lester, "only what is important jumps out at you. The blessing that AIDS has given me is that it's taught me how to live life with honesty and integrity. My relationship with God is personal, and I know I am a part of the Body of Christ. I'm free, not tied down to things or power or prestige.

Journeying with Lester has transformed the whole group. Ellen remarked: "When the only contact you have with AIDS is through newspapers and television, it dehumanizes the issue. With Lester in the group, it has been a real growth process for all of us, but especially for the men in our group, to understand AIDS and not be frightened. If a man is secure in his own sexuality, a gay man is no threat."

Several men in the group, including Ellen's husband, have found reservoirs of compassion in themselves that they did not know existed. Because they know Lester and he is a part of their community, they have put aside stereotypes and broadened their perspectives. "Lester has made a difference in my life because, first, I accepted him as a person," said Terrance. "But later, on a deeper level, I accepted him as a human being, even though I don't approve of his homosexual lifestyle. I don't gay-bash now. And I think something like the Holy Spirit made the difference when Ellen and I, together with another couple, laid hands on Lester and promised to care for him in his last days. That was five years ago." Lester is alive and living with the disease.

Lester influenced the group in other ways, too. The members hosted a potluck dinner to which they invited a group of Lester's gay and lesbian friends. Overcoming some initial unease, they wanted to be welcoming. Most of their guests had been alienated by the church and had subsequently left it. Even so, many of Lester's friends wanted to come back. The group had a discussion, read the Scriptures, broke into small groups for sharing, and then regathered as a large group. Community members universally agreed that the evening had been wonderful and that they had learned valuable lessons from their gay and lesbian brothers and sisters.

Lester's situation offered the small community of friends a choice in how they patterned their future together. They continuously choose patterns of presence, prayer, and inclusiveness. Their care for him became a love story in all its ambiguity. The gift was that it dignified them and added meaning and integrity to their lives.

Witnesses

Each of the stories within this community's story is part of God's story. Ann remarked: "It's one of the most beautiful roads I've ever been on. Bill and I work in several ministries. This is the group that nurtures our spirituality so that we are fed and challenged to grow in order to be more for other people. It's family. It's neat to be able to laugh, cry, and walk with one another." Continuing, Ann added: "I treasure being able to stick with it. I left the church and came back. You can see this community work, and to have the same values means a lot. Our faith has really been established."

Ed recalled: "I was in and out of Protestant churches. The Catholic church is the place where I found I could practice my faith. It's a lot easier to do that in a small community. I can be who I am, and it makes a real difference in our lives. Even though I'm not an evangelist, there are times at work when I can talk certain 'God talk,' and it's really neat being able to do that."

"I can't imagine being part of any church without being part of one of these small communities," said Barb, "because it would not be real."

As a group, the friends confess they have grown through many challenges but that the major breakthrough came at the retreat weekend. When they went through facilitator training in preparation for hosting the Buena Vista Tenth Anniversary Convocation (Buena Vista is a national grassroots organization devoted to the formation and support of Small Christian Communities), they learned more about the early house churches and began to understand them a bit more. They felt more closely akin to the people in Corinthians, Acts, and Ephesians. They identified with the messiness of those communities during Paul's time.

Sue remarked: "Most of the time when there is trouble or difficulties, you think that's bad. And that you're doing something really wrong. But you are growing, and it's part of the process. It's okay to have troubles. You get through them. And they make you stronger."

In the past this group looked at conflict as a sign of failure. The members are no longer afraid of conflict, and they see it as a sign that they are succeeding. In the meantime they are busy preparing for their annual retreat, this time including the gay and lesbian group. And until that next adventure, the Faith Family Small Church Community of Denver continues to sing their unfinished song and dance their unfinished dance.

QUESTIONS FOR REFLECTION AND SHARING

1. What touched you about the Scripture passage?
2. Have you ever been in a group that "made nice" rather than confronted issues together? If so, share the story. What was at stake? If the issue was resolved, how was it resolved? If it was not, what were the results?
3. Not keeping goals and expectations clear certainly created problems for this group. How do you keep your goals and expectations clear with one another?
4. As was the case with this group, there are passages of all kinds at different times and places in our life: at work, home, school, in the parish, and in the community. Share about a time when you had to let go of something in order to gain something. Where was God in that process?
5. There are many life passages we go through on the way to being community. Evelyn and James Whitehead believe that "whatever the passage, both human wisdom and Christian conviction tell us these transitions are not to be navigated alone. A central function of a believing community is to protect and guide its members through these harrowing and graceful periods" (*Seasons of Strength,* pp. 133–134). How do you feel about that?
6. Lester's admission led to a crisis, but also provided an opportunity. Are there any parallels in your life or in the life of your community? How do you respond?
7. What calls to ministry were heard by this community? Does this story offer your community any challenges to minister in ways you may not have considered?

Gracious and merciful God, help us to rejoice and be glad for every day of life as a gift. We thank you for all the people you have brought into our life, with all our differences, joys, and sorrows. Help us to attend to your presence in our everyday life. Amen.

CONTEMPLATIVES IN ACTION

The Mission Group
Dayton, Ohio

Holy Friend, you invite us on a lifetime journey with your presence in the people we meet. Help all of us to continue to walk humbly with you in the quest for a real Reign of God.

THE GOOD NEWS FROM PHILIPPIANS 2:1–8

If then there is any encouragement in Christ, any consolation from love, any sharing in the Spirit, any compassion and sympathy, make my joy complete: be of the same mind, having the same love, being in full accord and of one mind. Do nothing from selfish ambition or conceit, but in humility regard others as better than yourselves. Let each of you look not to your own interests, but to the interests of others. Let the same mind be in you that was in Christ Jesus,

who, though he was in the form of God,
    did not regard equality with God
    as something to be exploited,
but emptied himself,
    taking the form of a slave,
    being born in human likeness.
And being found in human form,
    he humbled himself
    and became obedient to the point of death—
    even death on a cross.

THE STORY OF THE MISSION GROUP

Dayton, Ohio, gave the world the Wright brothers, the pioneers of flight; the Watson brothers, founders of IBM; Kettering, inventor of the automatic shift; and Sister Margaret and the Mission Group.

Sister Margaret's story tells a lot about her determination and commitment to justice, both key ingredients in starting the Mission Group. Ten years ago Margaret organized a vanload of people from the Dayton area to go to Washington, D.C., in January of that year for a national meeting of social-action directors. While there, they had planned to visit their local congresspersons. Margaret prided herself on knowing her way around Washington. An unexpected overnight snowstorm hit town the day they planned their lobbying visit. Undeterred, and fending off the snow with her umbrella, Margaret trudged along at the head of the pack. The rest followed their leader with complete trust. Soon, definitely lost, she tucked her ego away, turned the group around, and eventually found where they were supposed to go. They did lobby, justice was served, and jokes about Margaret the fearless leader have stayed alive.

Margaret's commitment to justice got an undeniable push in 1972 during a thirty-day retreat. While she had always been concerned about social justice and had tried to instill this concern in both her high school and college students, her own activity for justice had been circumscribed by her duties. After the retreat she decided to leave teaching. "One thing I felt called to in my retreat was to be a contemplative in action," she recalls. "The retreat had wrought a real conversion within me. As a result, another sister and I began the religious lobby Network in Washington, D.C. We were animated by *Justice in the World,* a statement of the Synod of Bishops in Rome, which declared that the work of justice is a constitutive dimension of preaching the Gospel. We were inspired, too, by Pope Paul VI in his *Call to Action,* which pointed out that political action must be a part of our work in bringing about a more just world." Network has become one of the most articulate voices for justice among all lobbying groups in Washington.

During the busy days and months spent setting up Network, Sister Margaret kept her focus on Christian justice through her contact with the Washington mission group of the Church of the

Savior. The founder of the Church of the Savior, Gordon Cosby, came home from World War II with a vision of a church that would be interracial and free to experiment with new structures. He opened the School for Christian Living with one student. Side by side, Gordon and his one disciple explored doctrine, Christian growth, the Bible, and what gifts they might exercise on behalf of the church.

Soon, small fellowship groups met for worship, tithing, prayer, study, and corporate outreach. But none of the groups could agree on what its outreach would be. So Gordon set a new direction while comforting and reassuring the people through the uneasy transition toward mission groups. These groups formed around a particular mission but maintained an inner journey of study, prayer, and worship.

"Gordon Cosby's vision was always to integrate prayer, personal growth, and action for justice," Margaret declared. "Meeting with my group was a deep and convincing experience, affirming that we are called to grow spiritually in community and to integrate this growth with action for justice. Our mission group was ecumenical, and it was a powerful instrument in keeping me on course. One very helpful practice of the group was to examine each year the gifts and talents of each member in order to discern what role each person would play in contributing to the life of the community."

The experience in Washington with Network and the Mission Group led Margaret to her next job as parish coordinator on the staff of the Dayton office of the Cincinnati archdiocesan regional office of social action and world peace. Her major responsibility was to form small groups in as many parishes as possible. The hope was that they would integrate work for justice with personal and spiritual growth. She met monthly with groups, prepared agendas, and facilitated meetings.

The Dayton Mission Group

Early on, she and Roger, the Dayton office director, realized that they needed to prepare people to facilitate their own meetings and to take leadership roles in their parishes. "We invited a number of persons in the parish groups to join what we called the

Mission Group," Margaret recalled. "Roger and I met monthly with them and began the formation of a Christian community. Our meetings were very much like ones they would lead in their own parishes, even to some of the articles they would reflect on with their own people." The next year they formed a second group while continuing with the first. Later they had a retreat and joined the two groups into one, symbolically using yarn to weave the two together. "That was a real moment of grace," Margaret declared. "There have been additions and subtractions, but today, twelve years later, a faithful core is still meeting monthly."

The people of Mission Group come from different parishes and towns in two counties. All are professionals, and their ages range from forty-five to eighty. What holds them together is their common commitment to social justice, one another, and the social-action office. Specifically, they seek to promote social action in the parishes. "This is a frustrating goal," said Barbara, "because it's not easy to recruit people who are willing to devote time to developing it. Within the Mission Group, we've found support, resources, and the spiritual and intellectual stimulation to carry on."

The Mission Group doesn't have any delusions of grandeur. "We have a sense of the smallness of our efforts—the insanity of it all," laughed Pete, "and the bigness of the social-justice task. If we didn't laugh, we'd cry!" The group takes its mission seriously, but not themselves.

When They Meet

For three or four hours on one Sunday afternoon a month, the group gathers in the social-action office in downtown Dayton. It's a most appropriate meeting place because the single most important mission shared by the group is to promote the work of the social-action office. The members have served on just about every board, task force, committee, and commission of the office.

Sitting around a big table, the Mission Group has the building to itself. The people start every meeting with catching-up chit-chat. Then an extended opening prayer time includes reflection and sharing on the Scriptures, perhaps using visualization with Gospel stories, and usually an additional passage related to social teaching. Early on, Sister Margaret introduced the group members to consciousness examen. They continue the practice, though most admit that daily practice outside of the meetings is an ideal they have not achieved.

Two topics are discussed in each meeting. These topics include articles, books, presentations on an issue, spiritual formation, social teaching, or strategizing on a project that some are involved in. For example, in one stage of the group's life, the members spent time reading and processing M. Scott Peck's book *A Different Drummer.* When the discussion concludes, they plan the next meeting, setting the date, agenda, and delegation of assignments. Their meetings usually end with the Lord's Prayer.

Over the years, certain Scripture stories have come back for discussion many times: the parable of the mustard seed, the parable of the talents, Jesus sending the disciples on the journey in twos, and the parable of the blind man. Those stories exemplify not only the hazards and opportunities before any person but the memory that Jesus invites us to gather and sends us out in mission.

Faith in Action

The meetings provide support, insight, and encouragement to the members. The fruit of the meetings is action for justice. Sister Jean started a Peacemaker of the Month program in her school. She also founded the Jail Chaplaincy program and spearheaded the ecumenical effort with Church Women United to start a transitional facility for women released from prison. Walt participates in the Northwest Society for the Homeless. Their purpose is to provide help for women coming out of shelters.

Most of the Mission Group members belong to Catch the Building Spirit, a group of seventeen parishes working with Habitat for Humanity to build homes for needy families. Jan has worked tirelessly over the past decade to promote the consistent life ethic as a particular focus of social justice. And Sister Vera is determined to devote her retirement years to fighting racism, the death penalty, and political apathy.

The majority participate in the Dayton Peace Bridge project, which Barbara cochairs. Its aim is to promote racial harmony. Dayton is divided by a river that separates the majority white population from their African American neighbors. The Peace Bridge runs east and west and is used as a tool for uniting. Bea said: "Like most everything, it started really small about six or seven years ago. They have a program right in the middle of the bridge, bringing people together to get to know and accept one another. A breakfast for the children is served in all the schools that participate. A peace prize is offered to an individual who has contributed to peace. Sister Jean got the award one year. The gathering has grown larger and lasted longer each year. This year the celebration lasted through a whole week of activities."

Some members participate in Interfaith Action for a Violence-Free America. Others are active in Resurrection Building Bridges, a tutoring program for elementary school children up to eighth grade. The children come from both public and Catholic schools. Volunteers help them with reading and other subjects. A vital element is letting the children know that somebody cares about them.

The Mission Group's interests do not focus just on Dayton. Members have raised money and collected supplies to ease the suffering of their sisters and brothers all over the world and in poor areas of the United States.

Besides taking action, the Mission Group consistently tries to educate people in the parishes and involve them in service. The group has found many simple ways for people to be involved because most folks don't know where or how to begin. "Action begins with a seedling of an idea and a simple start," said Pete. "In my parish the social-justice group takes the time to pray and spend time with the Scriptures and to share ideas of how to bring about change. For example, we decided to serve food at the homeless shelter and asked for volunteers through the bulletin. Thirty people responded. People know they are making a difference, whether by making a meal, taking it, serving it, or interacting with the people. They know the basis of the service just through the little grace we say before the food is served. After a while we took another step. We invited the candidates for confirmation to participate with us as a service project prior to their confirmation. They have been doing that for years now. That little seed impacted thirty parishioners, and the life of many confirmation candidates over the years."

Gifted by Giving

The Mission Group has given a lot, but it realized that much has been given back. Barbara remarked: "It seems that we are into more things than most people we know, yet somehow we are less cynical and less burned out. The fact that we have stayed together this long as a group and have blossomed in our individual efforts tells us that Christ is in our midst. We feel that we are called to be faithful, not necessarily successful by the world's standards. We are gifted, gathered, broken, and sent forth. And Jesus said, 'I will be with you always.'"

Pete added: "Being involved in the outreach of social justice keeps you in faith, blessed with that Gospel vision. My company showed me that it values both me and my volunteer effort. They have given us seed money to keep the housing rehab project going. A lot of the skills I use in business, I first learned in parish work. Like how to motivate and work with volunteers in personal relationship. If you can motivate volunteers, you can motivate anybody."

Much to the surprise of the members of the Mission Group, they were nominated to receive the Diakonia Award from Buena Vista, the national grassroots organization that fosters and supports

Small Christian Communities. The award honors communities that have given outstanding service in promoting peace and justice. The members of the Mission Group were asked to reflect together on what they had done and to compose a profile of the group. Pete commented: "That gave us a chance to reflect on the good and bad of what we have been doing for so many years. We thought we had something good going on, but when we won the award, the recognition that other people also valued what we were doing was very affirming. When we were filling out the Buena Vista application, we realized that without our being aware of it, we had answered our own identity question about our mission: that each of us was called to different ministry and that our mission as a Small Christian Community was to support those different calls."

Not only has the service to the larger community given back many gifts to the group but members sharing their gifts with one another has been a blessing. One example of this occurred when they did an exercise to get in touch with their shadow sides, then dared to share that with the group. "Roger, the former director of the social-action office, was so touched," said Jean, "that he went around the table and told each of us in affectionate words why he loved each person and how beautiful each was to him. We usually feel our gift is less significant in the grand scheme of things than others affirm. The biggest gift we have is our extraordinary support of one another. This in turn empowers us to use our personal gifts at a higher level in the larger community."

A Time for Turmoil

No community is exempt from testing, even a community like the Mission Group. "Our trial happened," said Margaret, "when the archdiocese, pinched for operating funds, decided to eliminate twenty-three positions, including mine as parish coordinator. Decisions were being made by people unaware of what we were trying to do. The Mission Group wrote to the bishop and protested. Then began a campaign to raise money to pay my salary. They had reached the halfway mark when they were told that the archdiocese did not want independent groups raising funds, asking parishes for funds that the archdiocese might want to invest elsewhere."

After five years of forming the community, Margaret did not want to sever her relationship with it. She suggested that even though she would have to give up her role as parish coordinator, she could remain a member of the group. Roger, director of the social-action office, resisted. Margaret explained: "He couldn't see how I could let go of the leadership that I had been sharing with him. Roger saw the group as a function of the office. Yet I was already a part of the group that had grown into community. We in the group thought that the community should make the decision and that the community was not a 'function.' It took much processing and discernment. Because Roger and I were seeing the group from differing angles, it was a painful time for the group."

In the turmoil that ensued, everyone agonized over the situation. Eventually Roger resigned from the office. Margaret stayed in the group. Roles were distributed among the group's members. It took over a year for the tears, sharing, and healing to bring a measure of peace. Several people left the group; one left and came back. "Yet I think this was the event that made the group gel. They weathered the storm and came out as a more deeply bonded community through a baptism by fire!" Margaret said.

Looking back at the conflict, the group realized that its reconciliation began in an unexpected way. Walt recalled: "Someone who was considering joining the group decided sadly that she didn't want to join us because we were doing too much navel gazing and trying to define who we were! We realized later what a gift that negative comment was." The group had to review its priorities, reclaim its purpose, and move forward.

Keep On Keeping On

Reasons why the members of the community keep working for justice and peace are as diverse as the reasons why they started. Sister Margaret affirmed her call during a retreat. "I keep going because it's a calling and a commitment," said Bea. "All your experiences move you to do something. For me, turning in this direction was a process. When I graduated from high school in Arizona, I took a trip to Mexico City by train. Going down, through the train windows I saw children living in boxcars, half naked. We got to Guadalajara and saw a huge cathedral being built. People were outside begging. I was appalled. I thought, 'This isn't what the church should be. It's wrong.'"

Years later, Bea remembered her experience in Mexico when she received another wake-up call. One morning on her way to work in Dayton, she noticed a small, elderly bag lady. Seeing the poor woman in Dayton shocked her. She thought that poor people only lived in big cities. She dwelled on the sadness of such poverty when she attended the catechumenate program. There she encountered Pete, who was on the social-justice committee in the parish. He invited her to come to the Mission Group. Membership in the group has drawn her further and further into service.

Membership has also provided the support Bea needs to keep involved. She declared: "The support makes you feel like you're not out there by yourself. You are out there with people who have the same interests, problems, and desires. Twenty-five years ago, the Social Action and World Peace Commission formed. Before then, social activists were considered a fringe group of the Catholic church. Now this ministry is mainstreamed."

Even so, obstacles to working for justice abound. Pete confessed: "My wife and I, with our children, are taking a meal to the homeless shelter on Christmas Eve, and it will be very meaningful for all of us, but my extended family sees that as a distraction. What we hope for is that the educational moment happens so it becomes a win-win situation for all. The closer you get to God, the more evil tries to turn that around, I think. You get more obstacles in your path. The only thing that truly will overcome evil is love. And community is all about learning to love. Involvement can be really empowering, energizing, and life-giving for a community. Bringing people together to rub elbows does a lot more than meet an immediate need. Along the way, in taking actions such as serving food, building houses, and protesting peacefully, people learn about themselves and God. It adds depth to our life and the life of others."

The Mission Group believes that this way of being church is the only way to be. "Sure, we're a tiny, ragtag group, but look what Jesus did with his twelve," said Barbara. "Especially for lay people like us, this way of being church is empowering. Definitely, this group has changed us at home and at work! Each of us has become a little more courageous. The documents of the church are full of beautiful words, but the institutional church needs to encourage community involvement and discussion of social issues. We believe that people must experience smaller church for it to work. That is the promise of SCCs. The effect will be to strengthen the entire church. Small Christian Communities foster grassroots lay leadership. If those communities begin to reach out into their secular communities, the impact could be remarkable!"

In the final analysis, Margaret said: "Every member of the group is involved in social-justice actions that flow out of a life of faith. I believe the Mission Group is on the growing edge of where the church is being called to be. What is remarkable to me is that the members are so accustomed to their way of being church that they don't realize how extraordinary and important their approach is. May they increase and multiply!"

Questions for Reflection and Sharing

1. What touched you about the Scripture passage?
2. What stays in your mind about the story of the Mission Group?
3. This group centers its life on action for justice and peace. Is such a focus necessary for a community that calls itself Christian? Please explain your response.
4. What small or large actions have you or your community taken to promote peace and justice?
5. How can family members and friends, even if unconsciously, sometimes be obstacles to being of service or to taking action for justice?
6. How can we expect our children to act justly, love tenderly, and walk humbly (cf. Micah 6:8) if we do not show them how by our example?
7. Knowing when justice is being done can present problems. Jan, of the Mission Group, offered this advice: "Justice is only present when there is love and peace. If you are doing the right thing for the wrong reason, it's not justice. The question to ask is always, 'How is this bringing about the Reign of God?' Unless your work is deeply rooted in Gospel values it will go off track." How do you feel about Jan's advice?

8. Even communities dedicated to peace and justice can be thrown into turmoil over control or membership issues. How can prayer, reflection on the Scriptures, and ritual help people to cope with these problems?

9. Reflect on this "Recipe for Justice" derived from the Mission Group. What truths and challenges does it contain?

> 1 converted nun who has seen the vision. Laity or clergy will do well, too.
>
> Add 8 or more who want to see it, think they have heard the call, but aren't sure what to try.
>
> Add alternately, 7 parts yeast: prayer, stubbornness, love, the Scriptures, faith sharing, salt, and light.
> Add commitment to the above. A lot. And often, until it feels right and looks right.
>
> Cover and let sit in warm place.
> Add equal portions, one to one, of sugar, spice, and lots of nice.
>
> Beat group batter until it sticks and holds together.
> Knead dough with laughter.
> Punch dough with obstacles. Let hot air out.
>
> Bake several years. Check often.
> Stick toothpick (brandname "Advice" or "Challenge") in now and then, to test.
>
> Baste with more stubbornness as needed.
> Rest your feet, as needed.
> Call friends if in doubt about directions—Jesus, Dorothy Day, Dom Helder Camara, Rosa Parks, Gordon Cosby, Thomas Merton, Richard Rohr.
>
> Set the table for thousands. Serve meal hot, with loving care.
> Pray. Be not afraid. Serve. Clean up any messes you've made.
> Pray. Be not afraid. Serve. Pray. Be not afraid. Serve. Pray.
>
> Invite friends to make the recipe with you!

Loving God, we ask you to hold in your heart all the people for whom we pray by name now: . . . [Pause]. Inspire us to be imaginative in finding time to help create a more just and peaceful life for all our sisters and brothers. Give us sensitive spirits to understand and value people robbed of their dignity. Give us strong arms to embrace and serve those in need. Give us brave hearts to confront injustice. Amen.

CHRISTIAN FORMATION

SSFRE, Second Sunday Family Religious Education
Eldersburg, Maryland

Holy One, you parent us all. Sometimes your children suffer, especially because they feel powerless or hurt. Help us to nurture, protect, and guide our children. Help them to understand you as loving and caring. And help us to be blessing as family for one another.

THE GOOD NEWS FROM MATTHEW 19:13–14

> Then little children were being brought to him in order that he might lay his hands on them and pray. The disciples spoke sternly to those who brought them; but Jesus said, "Let the little children come to me, and do not stop them; for it is to such as these that the kingdom of heaven belongs."

THE STORY OF SSFRE, SECOND SUNDAY FAMILY RELIGIOUS EDUCATION

At Saint Joseph's parish, adult religious education and the RCIA were built around small communities. Given the encouraging response to the formation taking place in those communities, people began to wonder if the same approach could be used in faith formation with young people. So Marianist Brother Rick and the staff decided to try a new approach to religious education. First they suggested a new name, Christian Formation.

Then Rick took the next step after thinking about his experience in high school campus ministry. "We invited all the kids to come. Cheerleaders, athletes—the whole range showed up the first night. We would point that out to them, that they were just normal kids. We always used the upcoming Sunday readings and did faith sharing in small groups. We'd take the story of the prodigal son and do a skit in today's language and terms. For instance, the son moved to California, dressed in baggy pants, turned his baseball cap around on his head, and had a pierced ear. The kids would take it from there. They connected faith and life. After a while I asked them, 'What do you want for this group?' They said, 'We want to double it.' And they took the responsibility for doing it by bringing more kids to each meeting."

Rick and some other parishioners decided to try the same mix of invitation and small groups he had used in the high school to initiate the change to family, small community Christian formation in the parish. "We started with the teenagers. We thought if the teenagers liked it, the younger kids would automatically get on board because we were saying, 'It's cool to be in religious ed.' The teens did like it! It was laid back and took care of their fears about being 'stuck' with the little kids. On a standard family night where people are typically split into two groups, where would the teens usually be told to go? With the little kids. By inviting and working with the teens first, they had an idea what it was all about and could get comfortable with their role before family night."

Once the teens had embraced the community model, Rick initiated the next step. He told the teens about family night and asked them to help make the parents and younger kids comfortable. He understood that to make family religious education work, cooperative teens were indispensable. "If the kids are not invested, then the parents are not invested. And everyone shuts down." Eventually everyone would need to take ownership of Christian Formation, but at the first meetings the teens had to help.

Every parent who inquired about religious education was strongly encouraged to come to three consecutive religious education evenings. Family religious education based on the idea of Small Christian Community was modeled at each meeting. Four hundred people came to family night registration. They were invited to sit in circles of eight, and they experienced a small group meeting. In the center of the circle was the word, read and shared. At each of those three meetings, the younger children were invited to do something—hold candles, sing a song, wave ribbons, whatever. Organizers wanted the word to come alive for the participants, so ritual was important. Rick asked the teenagers to take some responsibility by helping the younger kids to know what to do with the candle or ribbon. Rick said: "That way, the parents could also pay attention to the reading. Then I'd say to the parents, 'Okay, here are your options for educating your child in this parish:

A. The family model: $25.00 for the whole family to be engaged in religious education, plus $10.00 for each child. For example, a family of two adults and two children pays a total of $45.00.

B. The traditional model: $35.00 for each child for the regular classroom sessions. Money is not the problem. If you cannot afford anything, of course you and your child are welcome.'"

After the three meetings, parents could select which format for religious education they preferred. Around one hundred people signed up for the family approach. This group was divided into smaller groups according to the day and time that worked best for them to gather. A different staff person accompanied each group.

The styles of staff accompaniment were as diverse as the families. "I participated differently with my group than some of the other staff," Rick added. "One staff person met with his group and had all the chairs lined up in rows. He was in the front. People asked questions, and he gave them answers. At the end of three months you could see the group falling apart. It just didn't work because nobody felt ownership."

How SSFRE Works

Rick facilitated the gatherings of the Second Sunday Family Religious Education, or SSFRE, for several months to model how the group could function. The SSFRE started its monthly meetings with small things like making a list of everyone's birthday. The teens would announce the list of birthdays to the large group. "They'd celebrate and have fun," said Rick. "I'd constantly applaud everyone's presence. Nothing went unnoticed. I held up all the good things to the light so everyone could see."

Five years later, SSFRE is still gathering. The community of twelve families meets after the 11:00 a.m. Mass, once a month. The parents' ages range from thirty to forty-something, and they have an interesting array of careers: a chef, a dance instructor, a radio announcer, a horse farm manager, and so on. Families come in all configurations, too. Rick remarked: "We constantly affirmed families of all shapes and sizes. In one group, at least five families had only one parent attend because the other parent was either non-Catholic or not interested. And still, the one parent consistently came to the meetings. Everybody was welcome. We didn't refer to the other-than-nuclear families as 'broken' families." While some of the adults had taught religious education before, they all came together now to learn from and fortify one another as catechists to their families. Though occasionally a family misses a meeting, SSFRE is a priority. Families come because they want to. There is no obligation.

An Evolving Format

At the start of their community life together, from noon to 12:30 was for welcoming, mingling, saying hello to one another. Snacks or lunch was included because the kids were hungry. This was followed by a half hour of gathering one to one or in small groups for prayer with Sunday's readings and commentaries that Brother Rick had collected. Then participants commonly read a portion of the Gospel and broke into peer groups for another half hour of sharing around a simple question like, What does this mean in your life? Each of the following peer groups met in a separate room: teens; middle schoolers; students in grades 4 and 5; students in grades 1, 2, and 3; preschoolers and kindergartners; and parents. Two parent-leaders took responsibility for being with each peer group, but the parent-leaders alternated months so that they could be in the parent sharing group on their off month.

The parents' peer group time included faith sharing in small groups, a large-group session to discuss material from the religious education program they were using, and a business meeting. During this last part, Rick asked them: "How are you doing with family religious ed at home? What do you need to know in order to do family religious ed the other three weeks at home?

What do you need to do?" Issues were discussed in a large group so the participants could help one another through their wisdom and experience.

For instance, at one meeting, Cathy said: "It's hard for us to find the time. What do we do?" Marg answered: "We had the same problem. Then we started doing it in our family on Fridays. The kids didn't want to come home and do homework, and we could delay dinner, so we'd have family religious ed and pizza. It works for us."

The SSFRE sessions lasted about ninety minutes and were followed by fifteen to twenty minutes of family activity based on the Sunday readings. Rick recalled: "Having some large-group activities really helped bring the group together. Infusing activities into what was already planned was a good way to approach ongoing materials. Music, arts, and crafts helped, too. Then, during the closing prayers, the teenagers might do a skit, mime, or song, followed by everyone holding hands in a large circle to offer petitions and share in the Our Father."

In the early life of the group, each month's meeting was planned minute-by-minute by Rick and two other families, including the children and teenagers. They went over the Sunday readings and planned the gathering so that all of the peer groups were represented and knew what was going to take place. "That's where the kids would pick up on it if too many skits were being done in a row," Rick recalled. "And teenagers were intentionally asked to work with the younger kids because then they were invested. As the teenagers talked to the little kids about forgiveness, lightbulbs were going off in their own heads!"

Now, five years since the group's inception, the planning process is shared by dividing the large group into three subgroups called A, B, and C, with about four families in each. Each group takes a turn planning the monthly meeting. That way each group has a few months to decide what it is going to do. The actual planning takes place outside of the large community of families. The planners talk it through on the phone, with one family acting as the lead family for its subgroup.

Evaluating

SSFRE evaluates the process regularly and brainstorms future directions. The people and their experiences are important to them. Mike remarked: "I really like the evaluating process, especially because it heads things into different directions. It's not the same all the time." The evaluation, in part, deals with the following questions:

- What is it that we think we are assembled for?
- What do you want to get out of it?
- What do you need from the meeting?
- What do you suggest in light of the kinds of things we have been doing?

Neither the adults nor the children are afraid to try something new or different. Change is constant. They keep what works and toss what doesn't. Their evaluation on a regular basis lets everyone know that their likes and dislikes will be listened to and taken into account.

How to discover God and develop spiritually in everyday life is the highest priority of the group. Patty said: "I want to talk about the Scriptures and spirituality and how they connect to our ordinary life. It makes me a better teacher. If I am not enriched in my spirituality, I will be a lousy teacher."

The children tend to use somewhat different criteria to evaluate SSFRE. Eleven-year-old Sean said: "I like the refreshments the most. And I like meeting my friends there. They go to different middle schools, so we don't get to see one another a lot. It's really fun. It's only two and a half hours once a month. This is definitely better than religious ed where it's like Sunday School, like a classroom."

Six-year-old Mark likes to go "because it's fun. I like to be with Jesus. And it's shorter than school." Mary, age twelve, likes "being with people who believe in the same things I do and being with kids my own age who believe that Jesus really did give his life for us and that he'll come again. I like being in the group with my family, too, and getting to know other families. It's like one big family."

All the parents were drawn to the group because they wanted to be involved with their children in a family setting instead of a classroom. Parents and children model for one another the importance of family and faith. They live it. Said Tom: "The word of God is what centers me, and being able to share that with others and apply it to our daily life is really important to me. That's what attracted me to this group."

From Insecurity to Confidence

Early in the group's story, the evaluation picked up one issue, the solution of which has led to tremendous growth in the community. While the group has worked hard to become community, the parents wanted Rick to do more supervisory work. Even though some in the group were experienced catechists, they felt that they needed more input because they didn't know what the church taught about a range of subjects. "With a traditional model of faith formation, there's not much attention paid to our call and the responsibility we have to be in discernment," said Rick. "We take the information in like we are a piggy bank. We were given the impression that we couldn't know as much as clergy and religious, and that we shouldn't. It instilled a lack of confidence in people, as well as compartmentalization into 'Sister's job' or 'Father's job.' These people in SSFRE wanted information! My answer to them was: 'I prepare this for two hours! I have to research it, go to the library, and find other ways to inform myself. You can do it, too!'"

To show people how to do the research and construct plans, Rick convinced three families and worked with them as an unofficial core team to prepare solid material for the gatherings. They helped tremendously. "Part of the staff person's role is not to let people off the hook. But it's better when it comes from lay people telling other lay people that."

Now the parents research information themselves. In discovering the information they are interested in, they feel well informed. "The best situation," added Rick, "is using input of church professionals, including laity, and one's own research. It's a good balance and people can still interject some fun processes of learning. A fourteen year old said: 'I just love our gatherings. They're not too religious, but they're really spiritual.'"

As the parents' confidence continued to grow, Rick backed away more and more. He would both check to see if everything went well and call to support those who had taken responsibility. "It's important," he affirmed, "to let things happen when you're not there. It helps people learn. I paid more attention to forming the leadership than to concentrating on details."

A more recent evaluation process brought about a significant change in the monthly format. "We were trying to do too much," said Bruce. "There just wasn't enough time for it all, so we opted for more time and fewer things happening. We stopped the small peer groups as part of the gathering. I like this better because now I'm with my wife and the whole family." Their meeting format now starts with opening prayer and a large-group activity, then breaks into small groups of about three families each for sharing, followed by a family activity. They close with a return to the large group for common prayer and petitions.

But this new format could change after the next evaluation, too. Sixteen-year-old Chris responded to the recent decision not to have peer groups as part of the format. "When I was smaller," he said, "we did lots of family activities, and we had peer groups so that each age-group could be together. Sometimes the older kids would help the younger ones so the adults could talk among themselves. Then we'd all gather to say the Our Father together. Now we have small groups in families, not age specific. The planners try, but it's hard to match up families with kids about the same ages. The little kids tune out or the big kids get bored. And sometimes the parents are totally quiet so all the kids can talk."

Serving

Becoming more service oriented has been a process of evolution. "As we grow more comfortable with one another in the group," said Monica, "we feel more comfortable in taking on one additional responsibility at a time." Resurrection Farm is now a regular part of the group members' experiences. The farm was originally started by a faith-sharing group that wanted a project. The people started collecting pennies. When there was enough, they purchased the land. Now it provides transitional housing for homeless people, abused spouses, unmarried mothers, or those recovering from drug or alcohol addictions. Birds, animals, and earth are plentiful. It's a healing place as well as a close-knit community of faith. The people who live there work on the farm and participate in community meetings. They have to contribute to the normal workings of a household—to be a part of it, not just receive a handout.

Bunny and Bruce have four kids. Bunny is devoted to SSFRE. It makes her a better parent, nurse, and wife, and Bruce is always willing to help out. The other SSFRE families are active at Resurrection Farm planting and harvesting corn, potatoes, or onions, or just swinging on the tire! Rick and the families planted four hundred and fifty mums at the farm. When the family groups first went out to Resurrection Farm to extend service, it came from that setting of family religious education.

The mission of the parents is to model, along with their children, service as a way of life, not as an event. Service now involves all age-groups and demonstrates a way to serve in the world. Another service opprtunity is the Alternative Christmas Market run by Lyn, Monica, and three others. It helps to counter the materialism and consumerism of the holidays. Mike dresses up as Saint Nicholas. People from area shelters, other nonprofit services, cooperatives, and educational organizations set up booths at the parish. People go from booth to booth and pledge an amount of money as a family donation. Then they write a check to the parish, and they're given a card that states that a gift has been made in their name to the particular organizations that they made pledges to.

Many Different Gifts

The Second Sunday Family Religious Education small community has thrived in five years because, according to the members:
- They got to know one another first and had fun through socials, service projects, and going places together.
- They shared in groups of two, three, and four so that intimacy could happen.
- Everybody wore name tags.
- When someone was absent, the staff person did not call the individual. Someone from the group did.

But it is successful for a lot of other reasons, too. In the dynamics of community building, people have formed a sense of their own calling, their own power in the spirit of God. All have had a chance to share their gifts. None of the experiences have been predictable, and that has allowed grace to enter. For instance, one religious education group was preparing for Lent. The priest led the stations of the cross in the traditional way. But the SSFRE chose a more experiential way for making the stations of the cross. They carried a cross with them to each station and reflected on sharing questions that were relevant to their life. In that process each family sat beneath the cross and made plans for Lent.

"In the first year of the SSFRE," remembered Monica, "a family chose to be part of the group family sacramental preparation to baptize their child. Another family acted as sponsor for six-year-old Erin. When the special day came, Erin dressed in white and was baptized in something that resembled a wading pool. Then she dried off and changed into party clothes for the celebration afterward. Parents and in-laws of the SSFRE also attended! The entire group went to the church and took part in the ceremony. Through that sense of stepping out in faith and celebrating the sacrament of grace, everybody got a new sense of what their baptism was about. The families looked up their records, revisited their own baptisms, acted out skits, gave readings, and revisited both the tradition and how it was a part of their life. It brought us all together."

One family in the group included Sharon and her five children from England. Bunny was working at the hospital when Sharon's son Patrick was brought in as an emergency patient. She called the group. Everyone prayed and was poised to step in if needed. That was extremely important because the family had no blood relatives in the states. Afterward, Sharon told the group, "I knew you'd be there for me." When Patrick got well, Sharon thanked the group personally at one of the regular meetings.

Rick recalled: "Lisa, a Cambodian woman, made spring rolls and brought them to the monthly meeting piping hot. She was saying, 'This is something I can do, and I want to share it with you.' The families didn't miss the significance of that. People often think of gifts like joy, compassion, and wisdom. But this was a concrete gift, really connected to Lisa's life and the life of the group."

Monica reflected on what the community has meant to her: "We are committed to this way of being church because it is family centered. It can be initiated at home. We are sure that we're making a contribution to the future because we are involved in community service outside the group and are practicing an evolving model of church in the world—religious education that begins in the family. Family is an essential part of society, and Christian formation should focus on family as the basic unit."

Rick has moved on, but the group remembers him fondly. He was a gift, perhaps especially because he helped them realize their own gifts. The community continues to take ownership as a group, and the members continue to grow as parents and as family members. Most importantly, SSFRE lets the children come, for "the kingdom of heaven belongs [to them]" (Matthew 19:14).

QUESTIONS FOR REFLECTION AND SHARING

1. What does the opening Scripture passage mean in your life?
2. How would you compare and contrast this form of religious education and the religious education you had as a young person?
3. Do you think that parishioners rely too much on catechists to teach religion to their children? If so, why?
4. The four essentials of church are prayer and ritual, Gospel, community, and service. What does the Second Sunday Family Religious Education community practice well?
5. Rick clearly had a lot of faith in teenagers. How are teenagers treated in your parish? in your community? Why would they respond positively to the SSFRE?
6. What are the advantages of families doing service together?
7. Share about a time when your family reached out to another.

Gracious God, your son, Jesus, showed us how we should welcome children. He blessed them and prayed for them. His whole life modeled your love to the children. Let us learn from him how to be wise and loving people, especially concerned for the good of the young. May we learn simplicity and reliance on your providence. You are our parent. You embrace us as your children. May we learn to trust and love you. Amen.

SHARING LIFE AND SAYING GOOD-BYE

The Emmanuel Community
Sykesville, Maryland

Courteous God, forming community challenges volunteers. We often learn the best and the worst about ourselves. Teach us about community, just as you taught your people throughout the ages, especially through Jesus (Sharon May, as quoted in *Open Hearts, Helping Hands,* p. 64).

THE GOOD NEWS ADAPTED FROM JOHN 15:1–5

I am the true vine.
The Creator is the dresser of vines.
God cuts off every branch in me
that does not bear any fruit.
The divine vinedresser prunes the live branches
so that they bear even more fruit.
Through the word that I have given you,
you have been purified already.
Live in me, as I live in you.
Just as a branch withers when removed from the vine,
so you will wither unless you live in me.

THE STORY OF THE EMMANUEL COMMUNITY

Maryland has been described as a southern state with a northern accent and a penchant for cherishing Civil War history. Marylanders call their state "America in miniature" because of its ocean, beaches, and flatlands in between mountains. Maryland has the distinction of being the only colony founded by a Catholic, Lord Baltimore. Its Act of Toleration granted freedom of worship to all, an unusual freedom in the 1600s.

This kind of tolerance and freedom of conscience typifies the Emmanuel Community. Members are well-read, experienced pastoral leaders in the church. Most of the members knew one another before gathering as community. They are old enough to have had events permanently imprint their life.

Some years before the Emmanuel Community formed, Robert and Lori Fontana had made an impression upon some of the community members. Robert was youth minister at Saint Joseph's Catholic community. He and Lori gathered five couples together weekly for prayer and sharing. In the context of that experience, they realized the importance of sharing faith together in a small-group setting.

Those initial five couples experienced and recognized the difference between a program-oriented parish and a relationally based parish. The premise of this first group was that a parish is where people figure out that their faith story is part of the story of the People of God. They were also committed to the notion that all processes of formation should take their cue from this question: How can we help people relate their faith story to one another in daily life?

Forming

Seeds of the Emmanuel Community planted by the Fontanas blossomed after a parish Renew process ended. The parish Renew staff person was thinking about sustaining the small groups as an ongoing way for people to grow closer to God and one another. However, no process or program was in place for that to happen. At the same time, about forty-five people from various Renew groups had approached Doris and Dan, the Renew coordinators, to brainstorm ways that they could continue the sense of community of faith they had experienced. The brainstorming resulted in the formation of the First Saturday Night Group, to denote the week and day of the month. They met as a large community intimately connected with the parish.

The first half hour of the First Saturday Night Group gathering was for family time, large group prayer, and lots of songs. Then the kids had preplanned activities to do while the adults broke into small groups for sharing, although sometimes the families stayed together. It wasn't uncommon for the organizers to put three or four families in different rooms with a bag of old clothes for costumes and invite them to create a skit reflecting a Bible story they liked.

After six months of the large community gatherings, people began meeting in small groups at homes as well. About a year later, Doris and Dan noticed that a lot of people had stopped coming to the large First Saturday Night Group celebrations. When they asked people why, they realized that people were being well supported in their small groups and no longer needed the large-group gatherings. Dan and Doris encouraged them to keep meeting weekly, and discontinued the large community gathering.

Power in the Stories

The group of eleven people who began meeting weekly at Doris and Dan's house took on an identity apart from the First Saturday Night Group by first asking of themselves, "Who am I?" At each group meeting, two members talked about areas of their life from a list of subjects that the group decided might be good to include, like: Where did you grow up? In what kind of family situation? What kind of process or journey were you on to want to deepen your faith? What issues happened for you as a young person? teen? young adult? How did you meet your spouse? What is your family's religious background? What are your desires for your family life, spouse, children, church, God?

Dan declared: "It was an incredibly good experience for us. If it didn't scare people to death, every small group should do this as close to the beginning of their group life as possible. For some groups it might be a year before they would feel ready to do that, but I think if you don't, you get a false sense of who people are." Encouraging people to tell who they are seemed to be the right place for the Emmanuel Community to start.

From Group to Community

Once the group members completed the process of listening to one another's stories, they embarked on the journey to identify themselves as a group. "Who am I?" led to figuring out expectations people had of the group. They composed a list of words that described what community is. The facilitator would take those words and build them into paragraphs that described what they would like to become as a community. Only when everyone said yes to the mission statement did they feel like they were a genuine Small Church Community. Emmanuel, meaning God-with-us, seemed like a good community name.

Family Oriented

The adult members of the Emmanuel Community range in age from twenty-seven to fifty-five. They have children from four months old to twenty years old. Ed and Kathy have a grandchild. All the members live only about twenty minutes apart. Some are liberal and some are conservative about everything from prayer styles to where the church is going. Yearly incomes range from thirty-five thousand to ninety thousand dollars. Ed, Tim, and Dan are computer specialists. Kathey and Doris stay at home to care for their children. Julie works part-time at a day-care center, and Kathy works full-time at a Christian family restaurant. All are involved in parish life.

Kathey is part of the parish service team for Small Christian Communities and helps to coordinate ten to fifteen small communities for mothers. Tom's career as a youth minister at a local parish started as a direct result of immersion in his Small Christian Community.

The families in the Emmanuel Community tend to be goal oriented. Even though all of them have had troubles, they maintain relatively stable homes and lives. Their children attend better-than-average schools. Many of the families eat their meals together as a family, and most of the families have developed meaningful family rituals.

One family has a Saturday night Sabbath meal. Bread is baked on Saturday, and they have bread and wine during the meal. Feast days are celebrated this way, too. Even though the children are very small, they catch on quickly. The Feast of Saint Francis was marked and celebrated, starting with Mom talking about Saint Francis during the day. At night, during dinner, Mom and Dad forgot to serve the bread and wine. Katie, mouth stuffed with food, asked where it was. After the third muffled question, both parents were surprised and delighted that a three year old knew that a tradition had been omitted.

Another common thread among the Emmanuel Small Christian Community members is sacrifice. They are committed to making sacrifices, starting with their own family. It always involves how time is spent. From house to house, their highest priority is to honor through action the family of Jesus, Mary, and Joseph by making their own family their primary Small Christian Community. They do that by eliminating things that take them away from this goal. Members, parents and grandparents alike, have made deliberate, tough choices to keep their family as the priority.

Over the years the community encouraged members to cherish even the small family events as holy. Kathey remarked: "People who are thinking about getting married need to know that coming to the table together and saying a simple thanks is a start. Just sitting down in a quiet atmosphere with a cup of coffee, or with five or ten kids, are graced moments. Maybe even more than in the formal, polished, and perfect settings. I think when life is really messy, God is there, maybe because he knows how hard it is. He's the God of down and dirty, as well as the God of polished and perfect."

Meeting

In the first few years, the members of the Emmanuel Community concentrated on Gospel readings, using a few resources to guide them in talking about the Gospels, their faith, and how these related to family, work, and life in the neighborhood. As more children were born, the community began to meet the second and fourth Wednesday of every month, year-round, usually at Dan and Doris's.

Gatherings started with 5:30 p.m. dinner for the parents and all eleven little children. Meals were appropriately chaotic: parents doing table aerobics, up and down, getting this, wiping that, an adult arm reaching to keep a glass of milk upright, children talking all at once, adults trying to get a word in edgewise over the din.

After the meal all the kids played in two big family rooms with a babysitter in attendance. The adults met on the front porch or in the living room. With candles flickering, people sat on the couch along one wall and on a deacon's bench, a rocking chair, and two or three other chairs from the kitchen—all in a circle. Icons, a prayer book, and an open Bible transformed the coffee table into an informal prayer table.

The tone could be quiet or chaotic, depending on how people felt that day. With a collective repertoire of over one hundred songs, everyone joined in for about thirty minutes of prayer and giving thanks. The natural transition into individual prayers of thanksgiving provided a simple way of affirming the presence and support of God in each person's life and allowed the group to understand that.

At 7:15 p.m., the Gospel for the coming Sunday was read. One or two faith-sharing questions were offered, and the group stayed flexible in how it processed the questions. Often people broke into pairs and shared stories, especially about how they saw God in everyday experiences. Sometimes they broke into groups of all men and all women, sometimes they stayed together as a large group, depending on their mood. One time the facilitator said, "Since the reading is from the Song of Songs, how is your relationship with your spouse?" They paired into spousal couples for the sharing.

By 8:20 p.m., the closing prayer had started. People were lifted up in prayer and remembered by others in the group. The prayers usually concerned some topic that was talked about during paired sharing. The community closed with the Lord's Prayer and a song. Most times the kids joined the group to close.

Staying Together

Early on, Ed and Kathy were key forces in helping the group stay together. Ed encouraged people to call one another and ask for support. He made a commitment to call everybody every week.

They learned from Ed how to support one another on a regular basis. He showed them by example rather than by preaching. A subtle accountability helped to maintain a connection to one another outside the meetings.

Facilitation of the meeting was rotated among the group members. The facilitator gave community members sharing questions the weekend before the meeting. They tried to keep the questions and the Gospel in mind each day before the meeting. Some reflected on the questions on the way to work. Some posted them on the refrigerator.

A pastoral facilitator, or PF, was chosen to be like a pastor, a shepherd to the group. Everybody gave insight and direction to the group, but they believed that the Holy Spirit raises up one person through group discernment to be the PF who double-checks direction and focus and is the link to the larger parish. The pastoral facilitator maintained contact with the facilitator as he or she prepared for the meeting. This kind of direction and focus enabled personal sharing between the two people about insights from the Gospel reading of the week. It helped to maintain a flow through the year of theme, process, and focus.

The Emmanuel Community believed that a Small Christian Community can lack wholeness unless it includes some form of reconciliation. The members went on retreat after they had been together about one year. During the retreat a reconciliation service included discernment about how they had hurt one another and how they could affirm one another. They sat in a circle with towels, bowls, and pitchers. One person would stand up, go to another community member, and wash his or her feet. Then both of them would go into a different place in the retreat house to talk about how they had affected each other in either a positive or negative way. They might then seek forgiveness from each other.

"It was one of the most powerful moments in the life of the community because it gave people a sense that we saw, we truly saw, Jesus in the face of the other person," remembered Dan. "And we wanted to make sure the other person knew that we were acknowledging the gifts that were there. If we had wronged that person, or if they had wronged us, we wanted to make an opportunity for accountability and forgiveness, so there wouldn't be a wall or boundary preventing us from getting to know that person fully in a truthful way. Getting to the truth of what it means to be in an individual relationship and what it means to be in a community relationship was a high value for us. It showed us the essence of God's Reign here and now."

Everyday Connections

The Emmanuel Community resonated closely with the story of the disciples walking to Emmaus in Luke 24:13–35. In the story Jesus joins the discouraged disciples as they walk along. To help them understand the death and Resurrection of Jesus, he explains all the biblical passages that foretell of Jesus. Finally they recognize Jesus when they break bread with him. Just as he had been before his Passion and glorious Resurrection, Christ abided with them in the ordinary events of their life.

Even though the community members embraced this passage, the women of the Emmanuel Community had been particularly challenged in connecting God with their daily events. Some years before the group formed, Doris decided to make the difficult transition from working career woman to stay-at-home mom. Her life felt pretty crummy. Literally. Much of her day was spent gathering up crumbs from the kids. Her prayer life also felt like only crumbs, too—done on the run instead of during an adequate, quiet time. Her spiritual director encouraged her to develop a "crumb spirituality" by looking throughout the day for little bits of prayer. The other women in the community provided graceful support for one another and for Doris by affirming that it was okay in this moment of her life to have just bits and crumbs of prayer.

John's Gospel story of the vine and the branches reminded all the women to keep rooted in Christ and the faith. That reading changed no one more than Julie. Julie and Tom wanted to have children. Julie took numerous trips to specialists to see why she was unable to become pregnant. Being legally blind, she had to rely on Doris and others for transportation to the doctor. Sometimes every day.

Julie connected those trips, faith sharing, and the metaphor of trimming the branches as a way to talk about not being able to have children. With great courage and trust, Julie shared her experience of feeling cut apart from the vine, feeling that her body didn't work right, and how disappointing that was for her. Julie remembered: "At twenty-four years old, that's a harsh reality to deal with. Depression, anger with God, and lots of 'why' questions took over my life. I think the graced moments for me were when the commmunity just listened. I always felt better after I shared with the group. At the end of each meeting, they always offered intercessory prayers for us." Her friends also often offered their tears.

The story had a happy ending. Russia gave birth to their children. Julie and Tom gave birth to family. With the community actively supporting their process of adopting a boy and a girl from Russia, the homecoming was nothing less than jubilant. In that shared experience, they all recognized that community means supporting one another in specific ways, at all times, in sadness and in joy.

Serving

While the Emmanuel Community members did not pool their money, and they all had separate jobs, they gave hundreds of dollars to one another in times of need. They tried to take seriously the stories of the early Christian communities in Acts, chapters 1 and 2, who shared their resources, said the prayers, and broke the bread.

They gave time to fix or renovate things, construct house additions, and give of themselves in laughter and presence. Not only did they pray for one another, they actively helped. Dan described their commitment as, "I'm going to be there alongside of you working, painting, putting up a wall, doing drywall, spackling, or whatever." For the Emmanuel Community, charity began at home, in the base community.

The community members viewed as their first responsibility their family and community. However, they attended to the needs of others by asking the question, "How am I helping my kids to understand what it means to be with the poorest of the poor?" A Scripture story close to their heart was that of being sent out two by two in mission and service.

Some members went with their children to a local mental health facility to visit patients. Kathey and Tim volunteered countless hours working with Tom and Julie in parish youth ministry. Tom and Julie viewed their jobs working with young children and teenagers as outreach. Two or three times a week, they also worked with the local high school color guards who are part of the marching band. The adults helped the young people to see that they are good because they were created good, not necessarily because they marched well.

Times of Trouble

Many times problems arise in small communities, in no small part because of how each person's beliefs were formed and by whom. A crisis of beliefs happened to the Emmanuel Community, too. These were well-educated people. Many had attended Catholic colleges. They were skilled leaders intensely committed to the church. No one was a rookie. Nevertheless, for all of their efforts to do right in the community, for all the good that they had done for one another and for their neighbor, they eventually found themselves at a fork in the road.

The members differed as to the cycles of community life. Some rode the ups and downs in community life easily. Others believed that the journey should be pretty consistent, especially if everyone was following correct church teachings. One couple felt that it was their duty to point it out when others were not on the correct path. Grudges started festering. Each person pulled a wagon loaded with high expectations, dogma, theology, shoulds, corrections, and judgments.

Letting go of expectations and other baggage in order to accept or at least tolerate diversity was a sacrifice the group members could not make. Looking back, they wanted community, but only according to their own definition. "There was no desire to do the work of being involved in that commitment together as community," admitted Ed. Tolerance and personal acceptance were often absent.

Just listening to the noise of discontent left one facilitator's energy drained. "When the meetings disintegrated into shouting matches over theology and dogma," said Kathey, "it was clear that each of us as individuals could not empty ourselves of biases and baggage to really accept and embrace the others with all their faults as well as their good points. The gap was too big."

Female and male relational dynamics affected everyone in the community, too. "All of the men had incredibly dominant voices," explained Kathey. "We spent a lot of time looking at that together, and thought it was just that the men were extroverts and the women were introverts. But I was really struggling with that toward the end. Some of the men had been brought up in a culture and time when they were not taught by example how to see women and their opinions as valid and worthy of consideration. I'm certainly not a radical feminist, but it seemed that the men looked at women as secondary to them. Women provided the refreshments and looked after the children. When the men got on a roll in the meetings, they'd just go, and there was very little chance for the women." In short, the women felt left out. And the men felt sad. They tried to make space for the women to have an equal voice, but the group never quite made it to equal footing.

So, the Emmanuel Community decided to fold up its tent. It recognized that the members had all learned a lot and that they take valuable lessons along with them, wherever the journey takes them next. They are the first to agree with Ecclesiastes that there is an appointed time for everything. "We nourished each other," said Tom. "Now it's time for us to be sent forth to share what we have received."

Closure

To the credit of the Emmanuel Community's members, they did not forget their Christian heart. The friendships remain, although they are different now. "I hope it shows others in community that saying, 'We can't go on like this' is messy and painful, but necessary sometimes," Kathey concluded.

Before going separate ways, the community took time to celebrate its good times. The friends had an evening of remembrance and prayer as closure. Although some tension, sadness, and reality of loss all mingled, a simple ritual helped bring a peaceful finish.

The group members brainstormed the kinds of things they had shared in their six years together. The list came to over two hundred words on a large poster. The most important item on the list was the births of children. When they began meeting, only one child had been born to members. At the end there were ten children age seven and under. Other shared events on the list were vans that died, seventeen cars owned among them in seven years (almost none new), meals prepared for one another, babysitting jobs shared, New Year's parties, accidents they had had, broken-down cars, trips to Russia, Valentine's Day dinners, singing at other churches, concerts together, renovating houses together, moving people into new houses, building additions, going through pregnancies together, attending two retreats at Cape May and two Steubenville retreats, Buena Vista convocations, accidents in snow and ice when on the way to another couple's house, Epiphany parties held every year at Dan and Doris's, pool parties held at Tom and Julie's, three in the group involved in Men's Breakfast since its inception ten years ago, Ed and Kathy's twenty-fifth anniversary party, Winter Blues party where everyone came dressed in blue, community participation in Tim and Kathey's wedding, Tom's youth ministry career started out of the group, corned beef and cabbage dinners, seeing the pope together, the cabin in West Virginia, personal prayer challenges to pray for everyone in the group every single day, and walks to the huge local reservoir.

Going Forward

Each member was enriched by belonging to the Emmanuel Community. Dan commented: "How I treat my wife and children and the way I attend to their needs usually reflects my desire to be real and truthful in how I am treating people in general. The rest of the community has been impacted too. We are seeking the right way to be with others in trying to build a relational community, whether it's at home or in eight-hour-a-day work relationships. That's a lot of time to spend with a group of four or five, or ten to twenty people.

"If there is trouble with a person at work, I don't just try to sidestep the issue. I go to the person and say, 'Look, we need to work this out.' I think it's because of community that I am that way. I think the community has also shown me what it really means to gather within a larger parish community and be attentive at Mass. Now I seek out the people I don't know, not just by saying, 'Hi, how ya doing?' but 'Hi, my name is Danny. What's your name? How long have you been in the parish?' and things that show that I'm glad they are there with me."

Doris and Dan, along with others, are in dialog about going on together in new ways. They are exploring the formation of a group built on the elements of a Small Christian Community with a focus on family-centered, intergenerational religious education. It would be formation for the adults as well as the children, and would include church teaching, ritual, tradition, and sacramental preparation. They would hope to make all the elements experiential.

"Community was important to me because I was transplanted from out of state," Tim declared. "They became family for me. Sharing our faith story helped that along. We could see what Acts of the Apostles was all about, and we wanted it almost too much. We had a lot of preconceived ideas. People don't want to die to their own ideologies and theologies. I would recommend that people just start with a tiny kernel of 'This is what community is,' and let the Holy Spirit form the people and the community. I don't think we left enough room for the Holy Spirit's imagination."

Continuing, Tim reflected: "Marriage is a metaphor for community. In the five years we've been married, Kathey and I have been through a lot. I wouldn't have missed any of it. A community is like that. We want it to be nice and cozy. But that's not how change most often happens."

Kathey added: "We have to remember that the Holy Spirit was among us. It's the mutual support that hooks people into a Small Christian Community at first. But prayer, faith sharing, community life, and service are the fruits that make people stay in the group. It was such a powerful and fruitful experience that we are open and looking forward to doing it all over again. When Tim was considering a job in another state, we decided not to take it because our small community was such an anchor of connectedness. Now that connection is gone, and we are sad but free. Tim has accepted a job in Montana. We've already visited the town parish there. Renew has been there, but nothing was planned for when the program ended. There might be some potential to get some Small Christian Communities started. It's just a matter of time."

QUESTIONS FOR REFLECTION AND SHARING

1. What touched you from the Gospel reading? from the story?
2. Of the essentials of church—prayer and ritual, community, service, Gospel—what do you think the community practiced well? Why?
3. The community hit the fork in the road and went separate ways. In your experience, what sort of beliefs can cause such division? Does their crossroad remind you of any crossroad in your own life?
4. This community put family and charity within the community priorities. What are the benefits of this, and what might be the problems in focusing this way?
5. How do you build reconciliation into your family? your community? your prayer? Is it as important as the Emmanuel Community thought?
6. This community came to closure. What might be some useful criteria for judging when a community should let go and dissolve?
7. Why is ritual so helpful in closure? Share your experience.

God, who draws us to unity, "the bottom line is celebrating life and celebrating the gift that each person is. Each person that we live with touches our life, or makes us aware of who we are." Give us open minds and generous hearts to build community among ourselves and in our world. Form us as peacemakers, bridge builders—in short, people of community. Amen (Laura Libertore, as quoted in Koch and Culligan, comps., *Open Hearts, Helping Hands,* p. 68).

PART B

In Part B, four communities are profiled that have few, if any, direct connections to a parish. Indeed, some were started because the members felt alienated from their parish. Thus, most generalizations do not apply to these communities, except this one: they all have the four essential elements of church present—prayer and ritual, Gospel, community, and service. They have also discovered that community building with Christ as the focus requires abundant patience.

Members of these communities have taken their baptismal promises seriously. They have lively Catholic faith. They acknowledge that parish-based communities have a vital role in building God's Reign. They also believe that their way of living community as church has a vital role.

Because these communities do not have the benefit of parish structures, for example, a resource person to suggest materials for meetings, they must find their own methods of organization and resourcing. These communities must also discern how they will effectively live out the Gospels in the larger world. Some are centered on celebrating the Eucharist together, and others focus on prayer and ritual, Gospel, community, and service.

Through his work as principal researcher collecting data on Small Christian Communities, sociologist William D'Antonio has identified fifty-three intentional eucharistic communities in the United States so far. Many other non-parish–based communities exist quietly. Their independence makes collecting data about them difficult. However, being known is not important to these communities. Being faith-filled People of God is.

These communities all have interesting stories to tell. They show us, just as parish-based communities do, that God is active in these groups of committed Christians. Good is being done, love given, bread broken and shared. These communities reflect that the ancient tradition of house churches continues two millennia later.

CHURCH IN THE TWENTY-FIRST CENTURY?

Communitas
Washington, D.C.

Liberating God, we thank you for your presence here among us, and we pray for all those who could not join us. We also pray for our larger church community. We join together in praise and thanksgiving to you, our God, and we ask for guidance that we may hear and honor truth with conviction, compassion, and mercy. We humbly ask your help to be church in the image of Christ.

THE GOOD NEWS FROM 1 JOHN 2:20–21

> You have been anointed by the Holy One, and all of you have knowledge. I write to you, not because you do not know the truth, but because you know it.

THE STORY OF COMMUNITAS

Communitas is an intentional community centered on the Eucharist and rooted in the Catholic tradition. Latin for "community," the name *Communitas* was chosen to illustrate how the members feel about themselves and the world at large. They want the world and all peoples to be community. The Communitas mission statement names the members as a body of equals who come together to form a faith community committed to making Christ's Reign of justice and peace a reality in our personal life, our church, our society, and our world. They gather together to be on mission as community and as individuals.

Understanding Communitas requires understanding its roots at George Washington University (GWU) during the 1960s, that decade of great promise and great crises: the Cuban missile crisis, President Kennedy's assassination, the 1967 Vietnam protests that began with the October march on the Pentagon. In the midst of sixties' turmoil, a couple retired to Florida and gave their home to the church, which converted the house into the George Washington University Newman Center.

Martin Luther King Jr.'s assassination, followed by Robert Kennedy's death, added more fuel to the fire of outrage caused by injustice and violence. Vietnam protests on the George Washington University campus led to confrontations with police. Concurrently, Fathers Ed and Jack were assigned to the Newman Center. Under their leadership, the Newman Center became a community grounded in the liturgy, dedicated to social justice.

More and more teachers and graduate students gathered in the Newman Center community. People outside the university began to attend liturgies and take part in its outreach. Father Ed helped found the Center for Creative Nonviolence (CCNV). Many of the community members became active in it and continue today in organizations sponsored by the CCNV, such as the Zaccheus Soup Kitchen and the Zacchaeus Medical Clinic. At the same time, the Berrigan brothers, Philip and Daniel, also used the Newman Center for meetings where they taught nonviolence and met with like-minded people.

Multiple changes in the church gained momentum in parishes like the Newman Center at GWU. Debates over church issues like *Humanae Vitae* led to divisions and outright rebellion. By the early 1970s, Nixon had left the White House, and Father Ed had left the priesthood.

Newman Growing

When Father Jack also left the Newman Center to devote more time to his calling as a physician's assistant, he persuaded the archdiocese to allow members of the community to choose the priest who would succeed Ed and him. The only stipulation made by the chancery was that the priest had to come from within the diocese.

Father Cary was selected by a community search committee. He quickly realized that the community's strength was in peace and justice activities. He helped people add an interior spiritual dimension to the community. The community also advertised for a female chaplain. Gail, a recent graduate of Yale Divinity School, was chosen. Soon a resurgence of student participation in the Newman Center began.

In the late 1970s, the GWU students began to question the role of outsiders, wondering, "Isn't GWU Newman primarily for members of George Washington University?" The community, both students and non–GWU Newman members, decided to formally evaluate where they were and what needed to be done. Interactions between students and nonstudents, more than the outcome of the evaluation, convinced both groups that they shared common goals as Christians.

Even as the evaluation process was going on, several community members, with other nonmembers, formed the Association in Solidarity with Guatemala, thus continuing the activist direction of Newman. Two years later, some members of that group formed the National Network in Solidarity with Guatemala, which became a major national focus of resistance to the policies of the Guatemalan government.

A Turning Point

In September 1983, Father Cary requested and was granted reassignment. But this time the community was not given a say in choosing his successor. Father Tom arrived. He altered three central community traditions: dialog homilies, women on the altar, and shared decision making. In a move to greatly reduce Gail's role, she was no longer allowed to read the Gospel or to preach more than once a month. Dialog homilies, which were an integral part of the Newman Center liturgy, were permitted only on rare occasions.

Efforts to curtail Gail's role even further were met with angry objections from the community. Meetings were held with Father Tom. Then, without notice, he announced that henceforth, although everyone could attend liturgy, only the undergraduate GWU students could have a role in the liturgy and participate in decision making.

A Blessing in Disguise

Some community members had little optimism after Father Tom's announcement. Others saw the events as an opportunity for the community to define itself independent of formal church structures. A large group of graduate students and other people not connected to the university decided to leave. They would not accompany the community that wanted to form independently, and they would not remain at the Newman Center. Most of the long-term members of the community, however, decided to stay together in the group that evolved into Communitas.

Communitas council president Mike Flood remarked: "It is a real trial of faith to see a community destroyed by the very institution that should be nurturing it. In the final analysis, we survived as community through the sheer grace of the Spirit. It is no coincidence that Communitas celebrates its birthday not in February but on Pentecost. Just as the original disciples gathered together demoralized, we, too, gathered on that second Sunday in February, and our rebirth in the Spirit was no less real than the rebirth of that first Christian community."

Quickly, the regularly scheduled annual retreat was revamped as a time to reorganize themselves. The group hoped to gain a commitment to remain together for six months and then reevaluate. "During the retreat," said Mike, "power flowed back into the community as we realized that the decision to exist or not exist was dependent solely on the members' desire to remain together, not on an external institution. The Sunday after the retreat, in a show of solidarity, Father Bill came and said Mass for us. In one weekend the community had moved from demoralization to the joy of rebirth."

They were reborn, but did not have a home. Charlie Davis remembered: "We were at the Presbyterian Church of the Pilgrims for about a year. And in turn, Franciscans, Redemptorists, Augustinians, and the Martin Luther King Center all welcomed us and, as hosts, said, 'You can stay here as long as we are here.' When we went to a seminary, it was the first time we had been in a church in a long time. We realized we had stopped thinking of church as a building."

In April 1984, still seeking a home with the church, they asked for a meeting with some priests of the archdiocese to establish a relationship. They emphasized that they were a loyal community of the diocese but deprived of a home. The meeting was cordial, but no home parish was forthcoming. The diocese's relationship to Communitas became one of benign neglect.

Forming by a Little-Known Tradition

The members organized themselves just like Catholic congregations did in the early decades of this country's history. Up until the 1870s, local churches were most often founded by immigrants. Whether German, Irish, Polish, Bohemian, or French, they took the initiative. In response to their spiritual needs, people would rent a building or gather in one of the larger homes to pray and share the word of God. Then they would ask a bishop for recognition as a parish, help in getting a priest, and so forth. If and when a priest actually became involved depended very much on when they contacted the bishop. For many years and in many locales, these house churches depended on Jesuit circuit riders to come around and say Mass.

This way of establishing local communities like Communitas is also well-grounded in canon law. Canon lawyer Fr. James Coriden declared: "The church recognizes a variety of local communities of the faithful in categories such as quasi churches (mission churches), associations, and other communities of the faithful, not just parishes. I celebrate Eucharist with several Intentional Eucharistic Communities in the greater Washington area. These are not maverick, rebellious, separatist people just protesting. They are people of faith, gathered and living the word of God. That's our history as an immigrant People of God, and it's happening again."

So Communitas continued this tradition of a community forming on its own, committed to the church, but not dependent on it. When they knew that the community would not have the services of one priest exclusively, they decided to seek a pastoral minister. In 1985, the community's search committee called Maureen Healy, a Sister of Saint Ursula (a small intentional community). She had experience working in the base communities of

Zaire, but mostly, Maureen just seemed to bring out the best in people.

Communitas is an adult community. Approximately seventy-five people are active members, but the total membership numbers one hundred twenty-five. Among Communitas members are university teachers, government workers, religious sisters, and people who work for humanitarian causes. People join Communitas by first hearing about the community and then coming to liturgy. If they like what they experience, they come back. If they come back often, they are subscribing to the purposes of the community mission statement and eventually might become a member by filling out a form with some basic information about themselves.

The community elects a seven-member council to manage Communitas. If the community needs a special meeting, one third of the members can request one. Regular meetings of the membership take place every three months. Standing committees for social justice, liturgy, ways and means, and social activities direct the activities of Communitas.

Gathered at the Table

The weekly eucharistic liturgy serves as the foundation of Communitas. The community celebrates the liturgical year—Ordinary

Time and the major feasts of Christmas, Easter, and Pentecost—
and each celebration includes all the components of the Mass said
in parishes. Communitas also includes liturgical celebrations of
Martin Luther King Jr.'s birthday, Bishop Oscar Romero's assassination, Epiphany, Earth Day, and other traditional Catholic feasts.

Liturgy acts as the center of the communal experience. Each
celebration invites members to bring their daily experiences of
work, home, and the larger world to the liturgy, where it is shared
through the dialog homily, formal prayer, and announcements in-
terwoven with communal prayers for personal and universal concerns. The community plans each liturgy and the liturgical space
carefully. They especially seek to be inclusive. Thus, they sit in a
circle. It affords the people an opportunity to see and speak directly to one another. The center of the circle holds the table, the
paschal candle, and the book.

A number of priests who are members of Communitas take
turns as liturgical presider, but the liturgy is planned by the priest
and members of the community, who take turns in the role of liturgical minister. As many people as possible participate in preparation of the liturgical space. The consensus of the community
members is that they all celebrate the liturgy. One member declared, "With a conversational dialog homily, communal singing,
and participatory eucharistic prayers, we are all celebrants."

The community members' strong bonds to one another and
to Christ and the People of God is particularly celebrated in the
words they proclaim at the breaking of the bread: "We break this
Bread as a sign that we give ourselves over to you and to one another. We dare to accept again your choice of us as tellers of your
Story. Give us new hearts, new tongues, new insights, and new
enthusiasm so that we might tell it well and truly. May we bring
love and truth to all those we touch. Move us to be faithful and
full of courage in the face of opposition. May our sharing in this
Eucharist which is Jesus' dying and rising be for us the beginning
of new life."

Because all members of Communitas see themselves as pro-
jections of the community, all their projects belong to the whole
community. So they exchange blessings with one another during
the final blessing, bless themselves, and bless all the work that they
take with them so that they can bring it back enriched. During the

final blessing ritual, blessing is also extended to people and places of concern for the community.

Although the community appreciates having an ordained minister preside, it is not adrift without one. Once, when the ordained presider did not show up at the celebration, Bill D'Antonio remembered: "The lay presider for the day got up and said, 'Well, we're going to start the liturgy and we're going to go as far as the Gospel. We're going to read the Gospel and then talk about what we're going to do next!' The Scripture reading was about the distribution of the loaves of bread. One of our comments was that Jesus wanted to make sure that everyone got fed. So, we plunged ahead. It was a defining moment in our community."

After the celebration of the word and Eucharist, conversation and coffee are offered as the members clean up the space together. On Christmas, Easter Vigil, Pentecost, and other special times, they continue the celebration with a potluck meal.

Moving with God's Spirit

As Communitas moves on with the Spirit, tensions and issues will keep challenging them. For instance, "issues that Communitas continues to work on," said Maureen, "include whether to have a pastoral minister or not. My viewpoint is that we are beyond that stage. We are at the next stage in our development as church community, one in which everyone needs to assume the responsibility for community. It's too easy to let someone else's shoulders take over."

Communitas meanwhile continues to celebrate the Eucharist weekly, hold its meetings, and take action for the good of their sisters and brothers. For example, group members actively promote justice and peace through the Guatemala Center for Human Concern and the Quixote Center. And members give service through a variety of other ministries in the Washington, D.C., area.

Communitas has committed itself to be church for the long haul. The members don't know what that will mean, but they have enough faith to believe it to be true. "The Spirit is forever asking us to risk," Maureen concluded. "People have a tendency to blame structures and hierarchies, or to abdicate. It's too easy to settle back and be our own community immersed in negative reaction to what is going on in the church. If everything is negative, we are not church. It's a very demanding process, but we are making the way by walking. The Spirit creates and leads."

QUESTIONS FOR REFLECTION AND SHARING

1. What touched you in the Scripture reading?
2. The Scripture passage is not suggesting that a society without law is appropriate. While the Holy Spirit is in our heart and mind, sinfulness is still as much a possibility as grace. Share about a time when you followed church or civil law over love. Share about a time when you chose love over "law."
3. This community has a clear focus on celebrating the Eucharist together, though most of the members are active in service. What do you find appealing about this focus?
4. How did you feel about the evolution of this community? What resonated with your experience?
5. This community sees itself as church. What do you mean by "church"? Share a few ways that you as a small group or Small Christian Community are living out that meaning of church.
6. What have you more clearly understood or learned because of the Communitas story and your sharing with others during this gathering?

Faithful God, you call us to be caregivers of one another and the larger world that is the Body of Christ. We ask prayers for those who have no caregivers. May we discover them and share our bounty of life with them—especially the elderly, infirm, disenfranchised, lonely, and those who have lost hope. May we be the whisper that brings new life into their heart, mind, and spirit. Help us to be a sign of your love and presence. Amen.

FROM RAGE TO REVERENCE

The Community of Jesus Our Brother
San Jose, California

Let us remember that we always stand on holy ground, because our God permeates all of life. Praise to you, everpresent, loving God (Laura Thomas, as quoted in Carl Koch and Michael Culligan, comps., *Open Hearts, Helping Hands,* p. 33).

THE GOOD NEWS FROM MATTHEW 13:18–23

"Hear then the parable of the sower. When anyone hears the word of the kingdom and does not understand it, the evil one comes and snatches away what is sown in the heart; this is what was sown on the path. As for what was sown on rocky ground, this is the one who hears the word and immediately receives it with joy; yet such a person has no root, but endures only for a while, and when trouble or persecution arises on account of the word, that person immediately falls away. As for what was sown among thorns, this is the one who hears the word, but the cares of the world and the lure of wealth choke the word, and it yields nothing. But as for what was sown on good soil, this is the one who hears the word and understands it, who indeed bears fruit and yields, in one case a hundredfold, in another sixty, and in another thirty."

THE STORY OF THE COMMUNITY OF JESUS OUR BROTHER

Surrounded by the Vera Cruz Mountains rich with flowering perennials and lemons the size of apples, San Jose is home to the

Community of Jesus Our Brother, a community that has continued to bear fruit for more than twenty years.

Twelve families form the core group, but the whole community includes twenty-five families. Some have moved but still stay in touch. Letters and faxes are addressed to, "Dear Community." Members tend to be well-educated, representing many professions such as psychiatric nursing, teaching, and engineering.

In the 1970s, the community was a Bible study group in the flourishing Christ Our Lord and Brother parish. The pastor, Father Tom, took seriously the documents of Vatican Council II, particularly the ones calling priests to form communities of faith. He encouraged ownership of the baptismal charism through home meetings of small groups. The Bible study group was one of many nurtured in the parish. Father Tom came to the Bible study group whenever he could. He also provided materials and the process that helped make church and religion real. Christ Our Lord and Brother was alive day and night as a church with a peoples' voice.

In those early days, Father Tom involved group members and parishioners in the total life of the parish. He often invited the Bible study group and others to his mountain house. "They knew me in old, ragged work clothes," said Tom, "out there fighting the snow, building this, and working on that." Such times cemented the bonds between the small community's members and Tom.

The community retains fond memories of those early times, perhaps especially of the Children's Masses and the monthly Family Mass. Everyone—children and adults—was included in the planning and in the dialogs. In the summer, we went to the Oak Cathedral," recalled Kelly. "There were one hundred to one hundred and fifty people at a time. We ate, laughed, and worked. Then everyone gathered by the big oak tree and sat around on logs for the liturgy. The kids loved that."

Father Tom encouraged experiential religious education that prompted children to question and talk with one another. Most of the Communion classes were taught at home by parents. Tom came into their homes to visit and help, but religious education had a base in the home and small community. One of the community members, Dorothy, remarked: "At one parish, I taught CCD for ten years and the pastor never knew my name because the parish was so big. Here, at Christ Our Lord and Brother parish,

I had a sense of having the small Bible study group, people knowing and caring about me, and still not losing contact with the larger parish. It was good, too, because you had the talents of so many people. Parish life was my whole life!"

Upheaval

The parish and the small faith communities thrived. Then came crisis. Father Tom had been serving the parish while being married and having two sons. The birth of the second child prompted the bishop to remove him from his parish. According to Dorothy, "The community knew about his situation and accepted Tom. The hierarchy knew as well. Having served twenty-six years, Father Tom was out. No insurance, no pension, no hospitalization, no concern about a job for him."

The members of the Bible study group were offended by, as one member said, "the lack of common decency and kindness. It was such an injustice by the church in the treatment of one of their men. I'd feel the same if it was someone in business who was treated that way." They were angry about that, but they were further outraged at the suggestion that he could continue as a priest if he would agree to deny his wife and children.

Parishioners had accepted Tom's advice and help for years. Indeed, people from the parish still call and ask for his help, and he gives it. The parish had helped people in need. If anyone in the parish lost his or her job, the parish held fundraisers. Now most parishioners did nothing to help Tom because the official church had acted.

As far as the Bible study group and many others were concerned, Tom had left the parish but not the priesthood. As one member of the community declared, "He's a priest down to his toes, and we all know it." Tom recognized who he was: a maverick, a married man, maybe a pioneer, and certainly a priest. Now, given their loyalty to Tom, their anger at the injustice done to him, and their commitment to the Gospels, the Bible study group had to rediscover its identity.

After long deliberation the group members left the parish. Or maybe the parish left them. The parish was renamed Saint Anthony's, perhaps in an attempt to erase the past, or perhaps to call upon the saint that helps people find something they have lost.

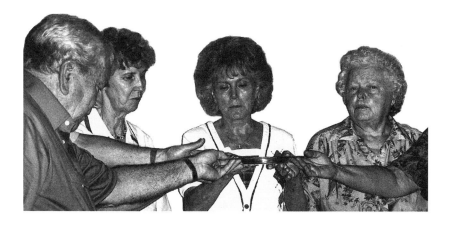

In the first few weeks after the group members had departed from the parish, they discussed if and how they would continue as a community. Anne recalled: "I remember feeling like the Apostles locked in the upper room waiting for the Spirit. We felt so fearful. Not certain if we were doing the right thing. We wondered, were we leading each other down the wrong path?"

Disunity and hostility divided the parish. The small community had supporters, but it also found enemies. Once Dorothy was pushing her cart somewhere between deviled eggs and angel food cake in the grocery store when a parishioner saw her and darted into another aisle. Dorothy would have no part of shunning or being shunned. She followed and started a conversation.

Dorothy's way of handling the situation was in some way symbolic of how the rest of the Bible study group was handling it. For Catholics of the late 1970s, they had made a radical decision. Most Catholics confronted church issues with silence or by just leaving. "People really didn't know what to do with us," admitted Dorothy. "They would say about our leaving, 'You can't do that.' And I would say, 'Oh, yes, we can.' Every Catholic has to grow up and take responsibility for their own soul without blaming someone else."

So the group set about seeking a future together. They began meeting in one place, then another. The restaurant they met at burned down, so they started meeting in homes. Gathering was the easy part. They were already a community. But they missed the parish and the pastor that they loved.

Now What?

Having moved out of the orbit of parish life, the group members realized that the study materials, rituals, and guidance that they had received from the parish were now gone. Their religious practice had been comfortable, joyous, and predictable because they trusted their pastor. Julie recalled: "We had lots of discussion about ritual, symbolism, and what was important to keep in order to retain our religious heritage. We knew we wanted to break bread together."

They also knew that their strongest need was education in the faith. They had relied on Tom to help them. He had the education and the imagination. They recognized him as a person of prayer and wisdom, someone, as a group member said, who tried to "emulate the mindset of Jesus, who didn't just preach, who walked the talk." In short, Tom was the ideal resource person.

Four months after their shaky start as a community, Herb and Anne, representing the group, asked Tom to facilitate an adult education series with them, and for his wife and him to become community members. Tom remarked: "I became the resource person especially because everyone else worked in different fields and didn't have the time. I wanted to be that person. It was my field. It's been a real joy for me."

Two months after that, someone said: "We haven't gone to Communion in a long time. Surely we will have Eucharist for Easter." Everyone agreed that they wanted to share in the Eucharist as a small community. Anne recalled: "Our most graced moment was the first Easter we shared. It somehow just seemed right, and it was such a resurrection from our fearful beginnings."

They chose to continue to celebrate life together, going on trips, caring for one another, and making liturgy special. That Christmas each family made a banner. Their liturgy became a celebration of a whole family of smaller families.

Around this time the community christened themselves Jesus Our Brother. They became a nonprofit organization, complete with a federal tax identification number and incorporation papers.

In the nineteen years since, the community members have experienced deaths, sicknesses, financial difficulties, differences of opinion, members moving some distances, and some testing of their values and existence. They know that struggling is part of community, but they have always worked matters out. Tom commented, "If you're going to be practical about incarnation and the theology of Jesus in the flesh, you've got to deal with the human nature."

Settling into Community Life

Discovery and recognition of one anothers' gifts helped the group stay together. The members recognized that diversity enhanced the group. "Leo brings his reality," said Anne, "Evelyn her years of wisdom, Bob his courage, Dennis his music and timely insights, Dorothy and Kelly their constant support. But one of the greatest gifts we give one another is simply being there, sharing ourselves, listening to and accepting one another." Long ago, anger gave way to love for Christ and one another, and hope that they can live more like Christ.

The Jesus Our Brother Community meets three times a month. A typical gathering looks and sounds familiar: an opening song followed by a reading, a man nodding off to sleep in the back, prayers of the faithful, the Our Father, the Sign of Peace, and Communion. But, of course, differences from the parish Mass are apparent: there are no vestments, there is informality, dialog after the reading, sharing of experiences relating to the reading, and preparation of the bread and wine by many hands. The collection goes to Tom, who distributes all of it to the community charities of choice, determined month by month. The community agenda is set by the group's needs.

Their quest for education in faith continues both in the regular gatherings and with an annual program financed by the community. The community provides funds for a volunteer who takes the responsibility to purchase books and subscriptions to Catholic newspapers for them. "In the small community meetings," said Dennis, "we've always had a theme, and dialog that allowed everyone to participate. It also challenged us to think and reminisce back to our own experiences through the storytelling. One of the best times was when we took up the story of the prodigal son. Four weeks later we were still dealing with it."

A recent bulletin gives some sense of what happens in the
Jesus Our Brother Community:

> Community of Jesus Our Brother
> Easter Bulletin
> Easter Saturday, April 6, 1996, at 11:00 a.m.
> Gardens of Sir Heater
>
> We will have a two-part liturgy: beginning at 11:00 a.m., we
> will pray and sing, read the Crucifixion story, and spend time
> mourning our losses during the past year; we will express
> hope in new life, sharing our experiences as we decorate
> the old wooden cross. Bring greens and flowers to cover the
> cross with newness.
>
> We will have a simple brunch thereafter. Bob is getting hot
> cross buns; J. O. B. (Jesus Our Brother) will supply Cordon
> Bleu from Costco and a beverage. We will make bread, as
> has been our custom, and we will exchange such during the
> offering.
>
> Note that we are meeting on Saturday, the 6th (so all may be
> with their immediate families on Easter Sunday).
>
> No gathering on Easter Sunday.
>
> On April 14th, we will gather at the McMahon home at 10:30
> a.m. for our usual Sunday liturgy. Subject: What do we mean
> by Resurrection?
>
> We will have a sign-up sheet at Bob's and a new schedule
> for all on the 14th.
>
> Enjoy the flowers and spring's new life!

Reaching out to the larger community is important to all of
them. Among other service activities, Jesus Our Brother Community is a member of Amnesty International and Bread for the
World. The community has adopted two children in Asia to support.

Metanoia

So, what do they have to show for nineteen years together? Dennis reflected: "When we had our tenth anniversary as the Community of Jesus our Brother, I thought, 'This is real.' And part of what made it real was because Tom was really human. Here, the message that Tom spoke was love—the concept that if there was love in peoples' heart, it could turn the world around. Imagine that!"

Invitations to this kind of compassionate love have come from most of the JOB members. The daughter in one family was having a child out of wedlock. The community helped as it could, so that the child became like the community's baby. Then, the mother of the same family couldn't go home to her mother's funeral. Knowing what a loss that was for her, the community had a memorial ceremony on Easter Sunday at a member's home. "The grandkids got up and spoke about their grandmother," said Tom. "It was a gift for the community to be allowed to do that. We continued to do that with other funerals. At a large parish Sunday Mass, people are prayed for, but you don't enter into their personal life. You can only do that in a small community where you know and understand one another."

Evolving, Growing

After the long years, life together still evolves. Dennis declared: "We're not in the same place theologically or socially as we have been at any other point in time. We started out looking like a church outside a church. It was sort of a transplant operation. Now we have a freer format while we have preserved a core liturgy over the years. We've come a long way in how we look at the Scriptures, and in what we believe individually and collectively."

The members have learned what they need to be, what their focus is. Fundamentally, they seek to live like the early Christian communities. Larry reflected: "They formed small groups around a focus or an individual, met in homes, celebrated Eucharist, and were very diverse. As best I can understand it, they didn't feel like they were separating from the churches and synagogues that existed at that time. And what I see is that sense right now. We are not trying to separate from the Catholic church, but expecting to become one large family in the future again."

The community certainly considers itself Catholic. The members view their rejection by church authorities to be unfortunate, because small communities like theirs have a lot to offer the church. As Leo admitted, "The church doesn't even recognize these groups, and the people in the small groups haven't seen a way of providing feedback or bringing their own increase in maturity back into the church at large."

In the meantime the community keeps trying to care for one another and build community. When Bob was sick, different families took dinner over every night, cleaned his house, and looked after him. When another person was ill, a spaghetti dinner was held to raise funds so that he could live for one month with no salary. Kelly just had double bypass surgery. Community members were there.

The Community of Jesus Our Brother is joyful about its community, but sad that going to the larger church for weddings and other occasions doesn't hold the same meaning. The group members still feel a sense of loss that touches the heart of what it means to belong. Anne declared: "We still have connections with our friends there. Dialog, forgiveness, and resolution have to be part of all communities much more than who is right or wrong."

"Everybody longs to belong," said Dorothy. "We knew all those people. We went to dances and parties together. We celebrated all the life events together. For us, this is the way to be community as church, and it's sad that there is a price to pay for that." Even so, the price that they have paid has brought a harvest of riches. "Now people from the parish come up to me and are eager to talk," Dorothy concluded. "Over the last nineteen years, they have heard the word 'community' more. When we left, people couldn't understand what happened to us, but didn't ask. Now they ask."

QUESTIONS FOR REFLECTION AND SHARING

1. What touched you from the Jesus Our Brother Community's story?
2. What have you done together as a group that helped you to get to know one another better?
3. If the door to your church had a sign, "Closed until further notice. No priest available," what would you do as an individual? as a family? as a Small Christian Community?
4. The Scripture passage from Matthew 13:18–23 is about the sower. What kind of ground are you when seed is sown? rocky? thorny? rich soil? What kind of soil is your community? Share about a time when something of God took root in you.
5. In the story Dorothy declares, "Every Catholic has to grow up and take responsibility for their own soul without blaming someone else." Is this true? Why or why not?
6. Is the price that the group members have had to pay for their community too high? Talk about your feelings on this question.
7. After pondering this story, is the Spirit calling you to any action?

God present, thank you for all the signs of your dwelling with us. Open our sight, hearing, taste, and touch that we may sense your presence here and now. Praise and thanks to you, always-with-us God. Amen.

BACK TO THE FUTURE

House Church
New Orleans, Louisiana

We honor you, gracious God, as we gather, and ask your indwelling spirit to enlighten us with the Scriptures and the stories of today. May we learn new ways of being humble servants. We bring before you in prayer the names of those who can't be with us now. Help us to carry your word and caring love wherever we go.

THE GOOD NEWS FROM MATTHEW 23:11–12

The greatest among you will be your servant. All who exalt themselves will be humbled, and all who humble themselves will be exalted.

THE STORY OF HOUSE CHURCH

The nine-year-old New Orleans House Church is a lively crowd of about a dozen faithful who can celebrate well in this Mardi Gras city where jazz reigns, cajun food tattoos the tongue, and natives take their chicory coffee thick and strong. The House Church also challenges the dark side of the Big Easy, a city with pockets of abysmal poverty, rampant violence, and extravagant corruption.

The community began in 1986 after Fr. Bernard Lee, SM, and Michael Cowan wrote their book *Dangerous Memories*. Bernard was teaching at the Loyola Institute for Ministry, and people there were interested in starting a Small Christian Community.

As discussions about the community turned into action, Bernard laid the groundwork for what would become a community of equal members, lay and religious, women and men, non-ordained and ordained. In previous communities to which he had belonged, Bernard had always been "the Priest," the one who presided at the Eucharist. When he had to be absent or when he left a group, attendance fell. From this experience, Bernard concluded: "I recognized this as a high valuation of Catholics having Eucharist, but also as a pattern that generated a priest-dependency. So I decided that if I became a member of an SCC in New Orleans, it would be as a member and not as a presider. I did this, and the SCC was off to a start."

The House Church continues to maintain close ties to the Society of Mary (SM), but the community found its original home with and initial impetus from the Marianists. The Saint Louis Province of the Marianists had formulated its mission statement, saying that in whatever works the members were engaged, their true mission was the empowerment of lay people to take responsibility for the church. The mission statement also urged the Marianists to help in the formation of lay communities and lay leadership. As a result, the province suggested that Bernard explore starting a new Marianist community when he moved to New Orleans. So, when Michael Cowan and Bernard decided to form an SCC, three Marianists joined in the effort.

The House Church has evolved to include three types of membership or relationships to the community. It includes members of the Marianist religious community—both brothers and priests, members of the Marianist lay community, and lay people not connected to the Marianist community. The House Church was instrumental in forming and keeps close ties to the Jeremiah Group, a network of thirty-four churches and about ten Small Christian Communities that work to change unjust systems in the city and state. The House Church and each SCC have delegated a representative to help direct the Jeremiah Group, which works on three or four issues affecting the quality of life of people in New Orleans.

Shall We Gather

The members of the House Church average in the mid-thirties in age and most have extensive higher education. Among the group are two lawyers, a successful real estate executive turned singer-

songwriter, a physician, a pastoral counselor, a high school campus minister, and a pastoral care minister. Susannah is a graduate student in literature at the University of New Orleans and is currently coordinator of the House Church.

The House Church meets in a home of New Orleans Acadian architecture. A big swing on the front porch invites members to stop and rest for a while. High ceilings, big windows, and lots of plants help people feel at home. Members who are part of the Marianist community meet here every other Wednesday evening. The entire House Church meets every other Sunday at 4:30 p.m.

The role of presider rotates among all the members. The group spends more than an hour reading one or more of the Scripture passages for that Sunday. The reading is followed by a large- or small-group discussion. Some social analysis always plays a role in the discussion. Sometimes the presider puts together articles from local and national newspapers that tie into the Gospel and deal with positive and negative ways our society works.

The group moves from the living room to the dining room to share bread and wine. The ritual might be spontaneous or follow a plan. "Sharing the bread and wine is eucharist-like. It's not Eucharist with a capital E," said David, "but as an assembly, we think it's no less the presence of Christ among us. Afterward, we all grab whatever we brought for a potluck dinner, and we share a meal."

By about 7:30 p.m., people are headed home. While the meetings generally have the elements of word shared, discussion, bread and wine, and potluck, the order and manner of the meetings varies considerably.

"We're the antithesis of structured parish programs," said David. "But I would use a different term than messy to describe our community and the way it works. To me, if something is screwed down so tight that it cannot move, it's not alive. This community has a life and a heartbeat." The House Church works by consensus, so naturally it might seem inefficient or messy. For example, when the members weren't able to come to consensus about the name of their community, they kept on describing it as House Church. Over time, the name stuck.

The most important agenda for the regular meetings and for other times together consists in nurturing the relationships among members. Ed declared: "There's a connection of friends, one on one or two on two, that keeps us together. Individuals meet outside our community meetings for other reasons. And it's not usually planned."

Through rotating the role of presider, allowing for variations, and focusing on relationships, the meetings succeed in fostering and recognizing the gifts of the House Church members. Andy commented: "Because of our openness, people are invited to be creative when they prepare the liturgy where we break open the word in Scripture, then break bread and share a meal. So the use of our gifts speaks to the fact that we are in an environment that facilitates us using our gifts." One time David and Missy helped the group experience Jesus healing the blind man by blindfolding everyone during the sharing of this story from the Gospel. Another time, Mary Lynn acted the role of a dream catcher to help the group process their ideas.

In its mission of justice and social change, the efforts of the House Church generally mesh well. The group members work out details as they go. Their discernment process is simple. They ask, "What needs to be done?" and "Who has the gifts that we could use right now?" Then someone takes the responsibility for coordinating for a six-month period. This person coordinates communications about work with the Jeremiah Group, the retreat, the schedule, and so on.

Being Church with a Mission

The support the members of the House Church offer to one another helps them look outward to the larger community. Jack remarked, "We come together with the foundation of making the Gospel real in today's world, so we spend a lot of time trying to digest what that Gospel means." One of the ways they live out the Gospels is through involvement in the Jeremiah Group.

Bernard added: "People in SCCs care about the world at large, but often don't know what to do with that energy. The Cowans and the Marianist religious community invited collaboration with another SCC (the Community of John) in the area, and they were all instrumental in beginning the Jeremiah Group. It is a broad-based community organization that builds a power base among religious congregations on behalf of social-justice issues. We are affiliated with the Industrial Areas Foundation (Saul Alinsky) and now have about sixty congregations as members."

The Jeremiah Group has become a way for SCCs that are not parish based to connect and to know that they are not alone in the Christian journey. An example of this is a project the Jeremiah Group researched concerning where public education money came from and how it was used. At one meeting three thousand people showed up. The mayor and the superintendent of schools of New Orleans were a central part of the meeting, which was recorded on video. The meeting and the research into educational spending focused light on an important issue and increased the accountability of elected officials.

"I wish that SCCs could, and they can," Ed explained, "become a huge voice for social justice and systemic change, and I think that that is playing itself out, at least in New Orleans through the Jeremiah Group. Ten SCCs as a group make the largest contribution of people to the Jeremiah Group. That's more than the other thirty-four churches represented in Jeremiah. Even though these SCCs are made up of eight or ten or twelve people apiece, as a large group of SCCs, we can have a tremendous voice. If people begin to see SCCs as a way to create systemic change, then we can go a long way to making social justice happen."

A Small Bump in the Road

So far, the closest the community has come to a crisis was when they experienced some tension surrounding the question of whether House Church was becoming identified exclusively as a Marianist community. Contributing to the tension was the observation by some in the group that over half the House Church members were either lay or religious Marianists. "The House Church members were increasingly edgy over this identity issue," said Bernard. "One member is very active with the De La Salle Christian Brothers and finds herself part of the Lasallian charism. Another's spiritual history has been with Jesuits, another with Religious of the Sacred Heart, and so on."

Through discussion and prayer, the community arrived at a comfortable understanding. They came to three conclusions:
- House Church is not a Marianist community.
- There is a lay Marianist community, however, and its members belong to House Church.
- There is a significant presence of Marianist perspectives in House Church only because so many members are formed in that charism.

"I think," continued Bernard, "that having come to terms with these issues, we are stronger as both House Church and as Marianist community. There is still some uneasiness probably, but it's not disruptive of community."

Savoring Grace by Making a Commitment

Many of the graces found in belonging to House Church echo what could be heard in most SCCs. "I'm committed to this way of being church," confessed David, "because it is so dramatically different from a typical parish life. This has taught me a way to live. I carry the sense of these people and this community with me wherever I go, and that feels like real live church to me. To know that my community is with me has absolutely transformed me in such a way that I don't want to live without community again."

David also described that involvement in the community had been a great way of teaching his children about living well with others. "If kids grow up seeing people share, they will think that's the way people get along. For example, one day two-year-old Nicholas, the son of our friends, went to the closet and pulled out every toy. He proceeded to show and share them with our eight-month-old daughter, Cameron. If parents are living a sharing model of family and community, it will positively influence the children."

Graced moments also come in very practical ways. New Orleans is below sea level. When rains continued unabated for days, David and Missy watched several feet of water flood their house. Missy remembered, "We were in a daze and didn't really know what to say or do because of the flooding." David admitted: "And I was troubled by the notion of asking for help. A bunch of folks from the community, kind of without us asking, just said, 'We're coming.' And they came over and began cleaning the house."

Another experience of grace took place more gradually, but was no less transformational. An Australian couple with their three children were living in New Orleans and were active in the House Church. The husband and wife were raised Catholic, but had no interest in the institutional church. As a result of time spent with the House Church, they grew more connected as church and asked for their three sons to be baptized. Campus ministry at Loyola arranged to have the three children baptized with the entire House Church present. "It was a powerful moment," said Bernard, "knowing these people had come to a recognition that even though House Church is not connected to parish, for sure it's church. They felt enough to want to have their children in the faith."

If a new person starts to come to House Church, someone from the community calls and shares with them a sense of the House Church history and asks them to make a short commitment of about six months to help out. "The potential revolving door," said David, "turns into, 'Here's a key. You are welcome to it, but if you take it, it has with it some responsibility to share in the tasks of the community.' People live by that."

Ed stated: "There's a real commitment in the group because we all know we're not in an ideal community. We muddle through. We're not righteous about it. My advice to other communities is to realize and appreciate how difficult it is to have a community that feels like it is making progress and moving forward when everybody still has veto power over the direction of the group."

New Visions Forming

"Small Christian Community life is the future," said Andy. "I think that the SCC model has in part been the home to some people who have fled the larger institutional or parish-based church for a variety of reasons. They feel more at home in SCCs because they feel that they have been marginalized or pushed out of the mainstream institutional church. I'd like to think that the SCCs will have a positive influence on reshaping or regrounding the institutional church and helping to recenter some of its values, particularly about a discipleship of equals. And I'd like to think that the positive experiences in our group and in other groups similar to this will contribute as a positive, instructive model for the larger church. If they can see how effective it is, maybe they will learn something, as we have, and be enriched too."

Mary Lynn has hopes, too. "I would hope for the treatment of women to be better in the church, including the ordination of women." Bernard commented, "Vatican Council II says that when people gather, there should be full participation."

At the very least, the House Church is engaged in a constant re-creation of the Vatican Council II spirit. One of the members offered: "It is great for married people to feel a sense of being a priestly people, and to feel as competent as anyone else in the group to lead the community. We all feel that way, not from anger or self-righteousness, but from a sense of call and response to Vatican Council II. I see it as a window to what the Roman Catholic church can become. Lay people are dying to usher in the Reign of God, and they are finding that SCC is one place where they can do that."

"If I didn't have this House Church community in addition to my Marianist religious community," said Bernard, "I'd feel really deprived at this point in my life. I can't even think of a church without SCCs and take it seriously. In some ways SCCs are off center, but those are the places where new visions will be forming. They will stand the test of time."

QUESTIONS FOR REFLECTION AND SHARING

1. Share your reflections on how the humble servant is or is not a good model for what SCCs should be about.
2. Many other religious congregations have started small communities of one type or another. Are you familiar with any of them? How can these groups give good examples of building a small faith community?
3. What most impressed you about the House Church story?
4. The connection between the House Church and the Jeremiah Group presents an interesting model of the mission of justice. Have you experienced any similar relationships between communities? What advantages does such a connection have? What are the possibilities for your community to form such alliances?
5. Bernard said, "People in SCCs care about the world at large but often don't know what to do with that energy." How do you and your community decide where to put your energy for good?
6. If you had a Jeremiah Group in your local community, what issues should it take on? What would be one small step to take in that direction? What would make you want to participate? What would keep you away, and why?
7. Ponder the hopes this group has for the future. Do your hopes have similar themes? Share your hopes about the future of Small Christian Communities.

Holy Friend, we ask your companionship in all our undertakings. Help us to be open to your many invitations to be humble servants. May we be your eyes to see, ears to hear, and hands to make a difference because of action taken in your name from the sincerity and love in our faith-filled hearts. We ask your blessing on all those here and on those who could not join us. Amen.

MISSION POSSIBLE

SCCs: Lodi and Acampo, California, and Chihuahua, Mexico

Liberating God, we gather in praise and glory of you. Help us to recognize that each person we encounter is precious. We ask your grace that we may be a reflection of a holy relationship with you and that we may be a harvest for others in the fullness of compassion, friendship, and love.

THE GOOD NEWS FROM LUKE 10:1–5

> After this the Lord appointed seventy[-two] others and sent them on ahead of him in pairs to every town and place where he himself intended to go. He said to them, "The harvest is plentiful, but the laborers are few; therefore ask the Lord of the harvest to send out laborers into [the] harvest. Go on your way. See, I am sending you out like lambs into the midst of wolves. Carry no purse, no bag, no sandals; and greet no one on the road. Whatever house you enter, first say, 'Peace to this house!'

THE STORY OF THE LODI, ACAMPO, AND CHIHUAHUA COMMUNITIES

This is a community with no geographical boundaries, no name, and no need for either. The members know who they are and where they are going. Pedro, Gloria, and the other community members have no need to tidy up, organize, or homogenize their Small Christian Community. They know that nobody owns the spirit of Christ. And they know that they share a strong internal network, from Chile to California to Mexico and beyond.

Pedro and Gloria have been working to form Small Christian Communities since they came to the United States from Chile in 1973. "We were looking for Small Christian Communities like in Chile," said Gloria. "Pedro met a person in the laundromat. They became friends and talked about the need for community. There was no Spanish Mass. They felt alone. Eventually a Mass in Spanish was offered. A different priest would come every Sunday, and more and more people came until it was overflowing.

"Then people began to meet in homes. Bishop Mahony—now Cardinal Mahony—from Los Angeles came to one of the meetings and was very pleased. He appointed Pedro director of Small Christian Communities. And that went on for a long time. When people would move away to places like Washington, Los Angeles, and Fresno, they would write us letters and tell us how they were continuing to form SCCs wherever they went."

The small core group of six, including Gloria and Pedro, is five years old. However, many small communities have started because of them. Attempts to organize the groups into a tight structure would be like trying to harness the Spirit. Said Pedro: "We don't have too many meetings. We just call one another, visit one another, pray together, socialize. That's more important than meetings. One time the people requested a retreat on Holy Saturday. They asked the pastor in the small town of two thousand. He said no. The people figured that the Lord, through the negative response of the pastor, was saying to have the retreat in the house. So they did. It lasted from nine o'clock in the morning until five o'clock at night." They have been having the retreat in a house for four years.

Gloria and Pedro try to prepare and support leaders. They visit and develop personal relationships. "The people get tired," said Pedro. "Each community knows best how often to meet—every two weeks, three weeks, or a project twice a week. There are about ten SCCs in the area. Each one tries to adapt to the reality of the place where they live." Reality to the communities means the current situation in their local area that makes life difficult and calls for social change.

Adapting, Helping

Pedro, Gloria, and other SCC members place a premium on adaptability. Situations change. People change. Pastors change. The question for community members always is, What is happening with the people and what is the Holy Spirit calling us to do? Pedro explained: "In the meetings, you have to see the reality of life around you. The "Observe, Judge, Act" method of evaluating and processing has to be there to really facilitate change of the social fabric. You must see the reality, talk about it, reflect a similar situation. Here in the United States, reality is people out of work, persecution of immigrants, and only a small economic middle class left. It's almost two classes now—the poor and the rich."

The reality for many people in the Hispanic community is that they shy away from getting involved in social issues because of fear. Gloria has found a way to establish trusting relationships to help people feel secure enough to get involved. She volunteers as a teacher of citizenship classes. Once people obtain citizenship, they feel more secure. Then they are more likely to get involved. "The Observe, Judge, Act process worked in one small community meeting as we started talking about a sanctuary situation," Gloria recounted. "Refugees coming from Latin America, especially Guatemalans, were having such a hard time establishing themselves. The result was that the group found two trailers for rent. To raise money, we started having breakfast every Sunday after all the Masses at Saint Ann's."

"We saved the money," she continued, "and bought the two trailers for the refugees to use until they got on their feet and found jobs. Then they could move. I wrote a paper announcing sanctuary and gave it to all the members of the community to sign. Then I had the paper publicized so no one, including the police, could come in and remove them from the trailers. That's how the first community started. There was a need. Now those families are dispersed. Some are in Florida, some in Washington, some in Stockton, California. They are doing very well.

"After that, we continued to use the trailers for the farm workers. Gilberto and Raymundo found a group of young men who were living in squalid conditions, all in one room with no water. Gilberto and Raymundo brought them here to live in the trailer for a while, and people went to the authorities to protest about the living conditions where the young men had been staying."

Gilberto offered another instance in which the community acted in response to a crisis. A serious food shortage threatened poor people in Lockford, California. "That's hard to understand when California is one of the richest states in the union," Gilberto admitted. He continued: "The SCCs pulled together and set up a food bank. Small Christian Communities are not just a group of people who read the Bible and start singing alleluia! No. They have to have a lot of action in necessary ways to help others. As the Holy Spirit works among you, there is almost an impatience to do something positive. An agenda, an urgency, a seriousness is mixed with laughter and shared meals. It is the movement of the Spirit that you as a group are listening to."

Members of these communities clearly understand that when they must deal with issues like health, jobs, and so on, joining with other groups, involving as many people as possible, makes an enormous difference. Nevertheless, Gloria added: "We're accustomed to making people do what we want, not what Jesus wants. But Jesus is not like that. He invites and welcomes everybody. Some get his message and some don't."

Reviving a Church

This small community takes action when called for, and it also nurtures its faith in other ways. For Lourdes, "reading the Bible alone is one thing, but reading it with other people really helped me to see different viewpoints and to discover a new meaning of life." Gilberto believes that "SCC helps us to learn about Christ and how to respect one another." "My family," said Maria, "started really knowing God through the Bible and sharing with people."

Pedro continued: "We are not alone. Without our SCC, I would feel alone. We became friends for good and for bad. This is our reality. Firm conviction. That is the Catholic religion. It's not magic—like drinking holy water or fancy things. It is 'Love one another and help one another.' We discovered that we are brothers and sisters, and that we have one God. All of us change with an SCC. When I first met Raul, it was like looking through this make-believe telescope. My view was limited. Now I see him differently, and I see Maria differently. She is not the same person I knew six years ago.

"I am a different person, too. I learned a lot from my Mexican friends. I came from Chile, and they are helping me to new understandings. They teach me how to be family, how to be open and receive hospitality at their houses. I can go into any of their houses and have a little food. I learn a lot of faith because Mexicans have a lot of faith. I am sure that all of us are trying to be the Good Shepherd and bring the word of God to others." Raymundo declared that "SCC is reviving a church where we can all form the same body of Christ."

Gathering to Celebrate

Over the years, more people have become part of all the SCCs around Lodi and Acampo. Rituals and traditions have become essential facets of their communities. For example, the people make a yearly *paseo,* or pilgrimage. One hundred or more people come together to eat, pray, and meet new people. This practice has continued every year for the last seven years. For some people it's the only time they meet. "More people come every year and ask about church, get to know one another outside church," said Pedro. "People are interested in church as a way of life outside of the parish. It is very good for families. The kids start learning the values of the family, and of a small community. They see and build relationships between family and an SCC, and they see how one helps the other."

Lourdes said: "They experience a *comunidad de familia.* It helps everyone to be united together." To Gilberto, the *paseo* models family as the domestic church, and *comunidades* as the larger family. His family and he learned from the small community how to serve beyond family and the SCC. He commented, "And it really helps your kids to grow up more Christian, together with the family."

Certainly one of the central customs in the community is the celebration of Our Lady of Guadalupe on 12 December. Our Lady of Guadalupe appeared to Juan Diego, a poor native of Mexico. By doing so, she affirmed the goodness and the dignity of all common people. Our Lady even wore *la cinta de embarazada,* a band decorating the dress she wore that was the traditional sign of pregnancy in the Native American world. Mary is the contemporary link to other faiths. Even Pentecostal churches use Our Lady of Guadalupe statues because so many Mexicans have devotion to her.

We Are Really Free

Small Christian Community helps people to be church in its smallest unit. It supplies a sense of intimacy lacking in the large Catholic congregations. Members noted that developing relationships is a key benefit of SCCs. "SCC is not a movement, a group, or an institution. It is a community open to anyone," Gloria said. "I think about the Letters of Saint Paul. He talks about how they gather, eat together, and stay in communion. They are happy."

Community members believe that people seem to fear that they will not "do" community correctly. Gloria continued: "But Jesus said, 'Be not afraid.' The first disciples were a motley crew. I'm not even sure they got along together, but yet Jesus chose them. It was almost like he picked them at random—a couple of fishermen, a tax collector, et cetera. The message is to include everyone—drunkards, the disadvantaged—everybody. If it doesn't work out, shake the sand off your sandals and go on to someone else!"

"We are really free," said Pedro gently. "We have the freedom of the sons and daughters of God. I explained this to my bishop, and he understood and agreed. If you are in a parish organization, you have to follow the pastor in everything. Some pastors believe they are God, that they have the truth, power, and control, and they expect you to follow them. It kills the spirit if people are following rules and regulations just to follow them."

This is not a parish-based community. The group was working with two other parishes, but when the pastor was changed, everything changed. So they are on their own now. They are a group of people who gather and are acting from their baptismal charism. It calls them to follow Jesus in communion with the bishop, but to be free in living their call, like Saint Francis of Assisi. He was in communion with his bishop but followed his unique vocation.

Members view their obedience this way. First, they obey God and their personal vocation. Then they are in communion with love for their bishop. They accept the truth of the Gospel and the teachings of the church. They are in communion with the faith through the creed. Next, when people need to confess, have a child baptized, or marry, they go to the priest. This is their commitment to obedience.

"Otherwise," Pedro continued, "we are free to do what we think we are supposed to do in response to the Holy Spirit. We are lay people involved in the church, and in the middle of the people, trying to bring the Gospel there. We feel it's important to preach the Reign of God. The church is important, but it is because it is a sign and a preaching about the Reign so the people can be of good faith. We meet together as lay people. We go to Mass every day. We are friendly with parish-based communities. We are not enemies."

Evangelization

The community helps people in practical ways, gathers other people into communities, celebrates important feasts, but also reaches out in evangelization. Said Lourdes: "The Scripture passage that comes to my mind is when the Lord sent the seventy-two out to other places. We are supposed to move out, too, and act as the early Christians did! That is the scriptural foundation from which the people are operating, but sometimes it brings surprises."

The communities of Lodi and Acampo sing, pray, use the Bible, and gather to celebrate. The personal faith development of the small communities gives many members the support they need to spread the Good News to other people. They find the large Catholic churches impersonal and often not inviting for Hispanics. One of the community members declared: "Here in California, each parish is a little kingdom with lots of money and lots of computers. The priests have no time to be with the people. One Mass on Sunday is fifteen hundred people. The priests are involved with the people who come to the parish, not with those who don't come to Mass." So the small community members go out on their own.

Several families decided to visit eight hundred families in Lodi. The first thing they did was to go knocking door to door.

David opened his door and remembers what happened: "When people used to come to our door to talk about religion and they weren't Catholic, I'd say, 'We are Catholics. We are not interested.' And usually, if people at the door aren't Catholic, we don't invite them in. To my surprise, one day Catholics came to the door and asked if we would invite them in. I did!

"They started to share their experiences of faith and what they were doing in the area. I was very impressed. They kept visiting me every week for six to seven months. I wasn't used to talking with anybody about the Bible or sharing Bible experiences. Either I wasn't ready for it, or I wasn't prepared ahead of time for the meeting. Little by little it started to build up, and I developed a sense of responsibility for being part of the group. I started to assist at the same church."

David was surprised because evangelization had been almost the sole preserve of Pentecostal communities. As a result, increasing numbers of immigrants from Latin American and many U.S.-born Hispanics have joined Pentecostal congregations. In ten to twenty more years, Latin America may be 20 to 30 percent Pentecostal.

Due to the evangelizing efforts of these SCC members, David and many others have gained a fresh understanding of Catholicism. They had grown up believing that Catholics attend Mass, say the Rosary, and do little beyond that. Because of the SCC, David concluded: "A real way to be Catholic is to visit people in their homes and try to get them involved in the community. I started to participate with the group. I've changed. I feel I have a big responsibility to the people around me. I was so impressed that someone came and knocked on my door. Community involvement is very important because we are dealing with people we know. We have the same level of education, same culture, same language. I think it means much more. You might move away from the community, but you take with you what you have learned and share it with others. It helps me to be a better person and a better Catholic."

The community has taken its ministry across from California to Mexico, too. Several years ago a pastor from Mexico was invited to California, and communication started between the two communities. Eventually, a group of nine members from the California church went to Chihuahua, Mexico, for a two-week visit. They visited eight small towns, each about eight miles from the other. One pastor served all eight towns, presiding at five to seven Masses on Sunday.

"It's crazy for one priest to say all those Masses and try to serve everybody in all those different towns," said Pedro. "So the people from California started forming SCCs in each town." When the priest was moved from the parish, the SCCs continued and are alive today. "We hope that more SCCs will start," continued Pedro. "We are going to continue to help them, and to put the new pastor in touch with the diocese of Ciudad Gusman, Mexico. There all the dioceses are working in a unified plan to form Small Christian Communities." These small communities continue to visit one another in neighboring towns and villages.

For the communities of Lodi and Acampo, theirs is a church without walls. "I see the Spirit working," said Pedro, "moving people to a new vision of church. It's something really serious. People are thinking in the future. It's not just people living a new way to be church. It is very simple, very humble, very small. They open a new path. The people stay in church through Small Christian Communities and do not just go away to other religions." Maybe they are staying long enough to see the unity of a church Raymundo hopes for, where "we can all form the same Body of Christ."

QUESTIONS FOR REFLECTION AND SHARING

1. What touched you from the Gospel passage?
2. What particularly struck you in the story of this Small Christian Community?
3. Of the four essentials of church, what are these small communities practicing especially well?
4. How do you feel about the statement, "Attempts to organize the groups into a tight structure of conformity would be like trying to harness the Spirit"?
5. This community tries to respond to real needs of the local community. How could a small community, your small community, begin to find out what the needs are where they live?

6. This community did not wait around to be gathered or organized by anyone. What are some things that prevent people from being more spontaneous about gathering Christians into community?
7. Catholics talk a lot about evangelization these days. These people do it, thanks in large part to the support of their SCC. What commitment to evangelization do you and your community have?

Holy Mary, Mother of Jesus, hear our prayers and petitions as you did those of Juan Diego. Help us to bring merciful presence to the people whose names we offer to you now: _____.
Help us to be good message bearers wherever we are called to go. Help us to be good fathers and mothers to the earth as you are, and good sisters and brothers in the one family of God. Hail Mary, full of grace, . . . Amen.

EPILOGUE

The Catholic church is a rich tapestry of diversity, tradition, and memory. Pope John Paul II reminds us that it is not finished:

> A rapidly growing phenomenon in the young churches . . . is that of 'ecclesial basic communities.' . . . They . . . become leaven of Christian life, of care for the poor and neglected, and of commitment to the transformation of society. Within them, the individual Christian experiences community and therefore senses that he or she is playing an active role and is encouraged to share in the common task. Thus, these communities become means of evangelization and of the initial proclamation of the Gospel and a source of new ministries. (*Communion and Mission,* p. 14)

The Small Christian Community is a central place to slow down and make sense of life in light of Christian values. People are looking to one another with the hope that by sharing faith and life together they might find the support and wisdom needed to be indeed the People of God. And so, in increasing numbers, Catholic Christians have returned to their roots, the Scriptures and the Traditions. There they have found the House Churches planted by the Apostles and nurtured by the early Christians. These House Churches kept the faith alive in the midst of Roman persecutions and all the hostile forces of Roman culture.

Today's House Churches help modern Catholic Christians keep their faith alive in a world no less hostile to faith, hope, and charity. The people in the twelve stories in this book are faith-filled People of God. They remind us all to look to our roots and to be the Church of Jesus Christ formed two thousand years ago:

> Peter said to them, . . . "The promise is for you, for your children. . . ." So those who welcomed his message were

baptized. . . . They devoted themselves to the apostles' teaching and fellowship, to the breaking of bread and the prayers.

. . . All who believed were together and had all things in common; they would sell their possessions and goods and distribute the proceeds to all, as any had need. Day by day, as they spent much time together in the temple, they broke bread at home and ate their food with glad and generous hearts, praising God and having the goodwill of all the people. And day by day the Lord added to their number. (Acts 2:38–47)

SELECT BIBLIOGRAPHY

WORKS CITED OR CONSULTED

D'Antonio, William V., James D. Davidson, Dean R. Hoge, and Ruth A. Wallace. *Laity, American and Catholic: Transforming the Church*. Kansas City, MO: Sheed and Ward, 1996.

Estés, Clarissa Pinkola, PhD. *The Gift of Story: A Wise Tale About What Is Enough*. New York: Ballantine Books, 1993.

John Paul II. *On the Permanent Validity of the Church's Missionary Mandate*. Washington, DC: United States Catholic Conference Publishing Services, 1990.

Koch, Carl, and Michael Culligan. *Open Hearts, Helping Hands: Prayers by Lay Volunteers in Mission*. Winona, MN: Saint Mary's Press, Christian Brothers Publications, 1993.

Lee, Bernard, SM, and Michael Cowan. *Dangerous Memories: House Churches and Our American Story*. Kansas City, MO: Sheed and Ward, 1986.

O'Connor, Elizabeth. *Servant Leaders, Servant Structures*. Washington, DC: Servant Leadership School, 1991.

Palmer, Parker J. *The Promise of Paradox: A Celebration of Contradictions in the Christian Life*. Notre Dame, IN: Ave Maria Press, 1980.

U.S. Bishops' Committee on Hispanic Affairs. *Communion and Mission: A Guide for Bishops and Pastoral Leaders on Small Church Communities*. Washington, DC: United States Catholic Conference (USCC), 1995.

Whitehead, Evelyn, and James Whitehead. *Seasons of Strength*. Winona, MN: Saint Mary's Press, 1995.

RESOURCES

Community

Baranowski, Arthur. *Creating Small Faith Communities: A Plan for Restructuring the Parish and Renewing Catholic Life*. Cincinnati, OH: Saint Anthony Messenger Press.

Buena Vista. *Small Christian Communities—What a Way to Go!* (video). 303-426-6622. Facilitator guide included.

———. *Small Christian Community—Basics in a Nutshell* (video). 303-426-6622. Designed as a primer for Small Christian Communities everywhere, this video serves as an integral communication tool for their formation as well as providing an enhancement to their ongoing development and support. Facilitator guide included.

Howard, Barbara, and Bill D'Antonio. *Ubi Caritas* (six-session book). Buena Vista. 303-426-6622.

Kleissler, Thomas, Margo LeBert, and Mary McGuinness. *Small Christian Communities: A Vision of Hope*. Mahwah, NJ: Paulist Press. Wonderful basic primer.

Lamb, Betsy. *The Big How-To Book*. San Francisco: PRCS.

Marins, Jose, Teolide Trevisan, and Carolee Chanona. *The Church from the Roots*. Catholic Fund for Overseas Development.

———. *Gift for the Present* (video). Buena Vista. 303-426-6622. Facilitator guide included.

———. *Insights from the Past* (video). Buena Vista. 303-426-6622. Facilitator guide included.

———. *Legacy for the Future* (video). Buena Vista. 303-426-6622. Facilitator guide included.

Mauren, Mary LaCourse. *Creating Communities of Good News: A Handbook for Small Group*. Kansas City, MO: Sheed and Ward.

O'Brien, Timothy. *Why Small Christian Communities Work*. San Francisco: Resource Publications.

O'Halloran, James. *Small Christian Communities: A Pastoral Companion*. Maryknoll, NY: Orbis.

Pelton, Robert S. *From Power to Communion*. Notre Dame, IN: University of Notre Dame Press.

U.S. Bishops' Committee on Hispanic Affairs. *Communion and Mission* (video and booklet). Washington, DC: USCC. 800-235-8722.

Service and Justice

Eichten, Peter, Michael Cowan, and Bernard Lee, SM. *Seeking Justice* (six-session book). Buena Vista. 303-426-6622. Excellent material for an established SCC.

Kleissler, Thomas. *Outreach—The Two Feet of Service and Justice* (video). Buena Vista. 303-426-6622. This video guides its audience in their search for the Scriptures' wisdom and prepares them for group action to facilitate change.

Vanderhaar, Gerard. *Why Good People Do Bad Things.* Mystic, CT: Twenty-Third Publications. Uncovers some underlying causes of injustice that we are probably unaware of.

Gospel

Calderone-Stewart, Lisa-Marie. *In Touch with the Word: Lectionary-Based Prayer Reflections—Advent, Christmas, Lent, and Easter.* Winona, MN: Saint Mary's Press.

Coleman, Lyman, et al. *Serendipity Bible for Study Groups.* Serendipity House. 800-525-9563.

Hollyday, Joyce. *Clothed with the Sun.* Philadelphia: Westminster/John Knox Press. Presents Biblical women in a new light.

The Serendipity New Testament for Study Groups. Mahwah, NJ: Paulist Press.

Prayer and Ritual

Baranowski, Arthur. *Praying Alone and Together.* Cincinnati: Saint Anthony Messenger Press.

Bergan, Jacqueline Syrup, and S. Marie Schwan. *Taste and See: Prayer Services for Gatherings of Faith.* Winona, MN: Saint Mary's Press.

Gabriele, Edward. *Act Justly, Love Tenderly, Walk Humbly: Prayers for Peace and Justice.* Winona, MN: Saint Mary's Press.

Mossi, John, and Suzanne Toolan. *Canticles and Gathering Prayers.*
    Winona, MN: Saint Mary's Press.
Rathschmidt, Jack, and Gaynell Bordes Cronin. *Rituals for Home
    and Parish.* Mahwah, NJ: Paulist Press.
Simsic, Wayne. *Garden Prayers: Planting the Seeds of Your Inner
    Life.* Winona, MN: Saint Mary's Press.

Incorporating All Essentials of Church

Good Ground Press. *Sunday by Sunday.* 612-690-7010. Inclusive
    lectionary-based material for each week of the year: prayer,
    the Scriptures, sending out in service.
Hild, Tom, and Michele Naughton. *Small Christian Community
    and Youth? Yes!* (video). Buena Vista. 303-426-6622. The pre-
    senters talk frankly about how and why youth are attracted
    to involvement in a small-group experience. Includes specif-
    ic support suggestions needed by today's teens to assist them
    in their everyday activities and faith-sharing needs.
Link, Mark. *Vision 2000 Series.* Tabor Publishing. 800-527-4747. A
    daily meditation program based on the lectionary readings
    for Cycles A, B, and C. Could be used as beginning and con-
    tinuing material for SCCs.
Loescher, Elizabeth. *Skills for Practical Peacemaking* (video). Bue-
    na Vista. 303-426-6622. Easy answers for anyone who has
    wondered what to say, when to say it, how to say it, and has
    felt put on the spot.
Moriarty, Robert, and Pastoral Department for Small Christian
    Communities, Hartford Diocese. *Quest* (seasonal booklet for
    SCC). 203-243-9642.
Saint Anthony Messenger Press. *Gospel Attitudes (Inner Action)*
    (six-part video series). 800-488-0488. Includes facilitator guide
    and participant magazine. It is a good beginning series for a
    parish.

Publications

Buena Vista INK. Buena Vista. 303-426-6622. A twelve-page newsletter, six issues per year, written by SCC members for SCC members. Includes ideas that work, motivation, spiritual guidance, and pages to copy and run with: sharing sessions, prayer, inclusions for your parish newsletter, SCC and Buena Vista news, and so on. Complimentary to members.

Acknowledgements *(continued)*

The psalm on page 63 is from *Psalms Anew: In Inclusive Language,* compiled by Nancy Schreck and Maureen Leach (Winona, MN: Saint Mary's Press, 1986). Copyright © 1986 by Saint Mary's Press. All rights reserved.

All other scriptural quotations in this book are from the New Revised Standard Version of the Bible. Copyright © 1989 by the Division of Christian Education of the National Council of the Churches of Christ in the United States of America. Used with permission. All rights reserved.

The excerpt on page 13 is from *The Promise of Paradox: A Celebration of Contradictions in the Christian Life,* by Parker J. Palmer (Notre Dame, IN: Ave Maria Press, 1980), page 108. Copyright © 1980 by Ave Maria Press.

The excerpt on pages 19–20 is from *The Gift of Story: A Wise Tale About What Is Enough,* by Clarissa Pinkola Estés, PhD (New York: Ballantine Books, 1993), pages 28–30. Copyright © 1993. All performance, derivative, adaptation, musical, audio and recording, illustrative, theatrical, film, pictorial, electronic, and all other rights reserved. Reprinted by kind permission of the author, Dr. Estés, and Ballantine Books, a division of Random House.

The excerpts on pages 43, 53, 54, 62, 99, 112, and 124 are from *Open Hearts, Helping Hands: Prayers by Lay Volunteers in Mission,* compiled by Carl Koch and Michael Culligan (Winona, MN: Saint Mary's Press, 1993), pages 29, 32, 25, 28, 64, 68, and 33, respectively. Copyright © 1993 by Saint Mary's Press. Used with permission.

The excerpt on page 73 is from *Seasons of Strength,* by Evelyn Eaton Whitehead and James D. Whitehead (Winona, MN: Saint Mary's Press, 1995), pages 133–134. Copyright © 1995 by Saint Mary's Press. This excerpt originally appeared in *A Challenge to Love: Gay and Lesbian Catholics in the Church,* edited by Robert Nugent (Crossroad, 1983). Copyright © 1983 by Evelyn Eaton White-head and James D. Whitehead.

The excerpt on page 153 is from *Communion and Mission: A Guide for Bishops and Pastoral Leaders on Small Church Communities,* by the U.S. Bishops' Committee on Hispanic Affairs (Washington, DC: United States Catholic Conference, 1995), page 14. Copyright © 1995 by the United States Catholic Conference.